Reflections From
A Strange Island

Woody Richards

For Jayne

Contents

Castaway

Lewis Carroll, wrote in 'Alice in Wonderland' that 'if you don't know where you are going, then any road will get you there'. I wonder though, whether we have a destination in mind or not, do we really have any choice about which road we take? It seems not, for we are sometimes unwilling travellers, drawn along by the unseen tides of destiny. To assert that we have some direction over our lives is perhaps to go against those tides and currents. To go against the flow is surely to drown in it, isn't it? However, sometimes there are places you get swept to in your life - like sandbanks that collect detritus upon them. This tangle of flotsam may stay snagged, marooned for a time until the currents take it further downstream to other sandbanks and other destinations. Some components of the tangle may stay lodged permanently or semi permanently; some may even become so tangled that they join together. The Island was such a place.

The Island was not some coral-lagooned palm-treed paradise in a blue ocean – no, it was an island formed by a loop in an English river which had been isolated by a channel cut at its narrowest part. There were no natives living there, it was a strange place populated by castaways from the world beyond. Some had gone to the Island because they realistically had no other choice, some because they imagined they would live their dream, some to escape a nightmare, almost all of them though were escaping from something, somewhere, or somebody, but once they crossed the single bridge to the Island they found a haven from the insanity that the outer world had become and they found in their own way a special kind of peace.

White swans with angel wing-beats look down upon this far country, where black crows drift in ragged flocks to feed on field or road kill, where the grey heron stands at the water's edge and the kingfisher passes as a bright blue arrow.

The Island lies a mile from the nearest village, which is itself miles from anywhere. This is an area that consists of depressingly flat farmland, the soil rich and as black as soot, screened now and then from the wind by soldierly rows of trees. This is an artificial landscape. Not so far back in time this was an inland sea that was gradually drained - first by the Romans, then the Dutch – who knew a thing or two about drainage. Dykes were built, ditches were dug, windmills patiently pumped, the course of the rivers were even reversed in some cases. Over time the waters were expelled, the land slowly reclaimed. Now there are few houses here more than one storey high and such towns as exist live upon what were once islands in that inland sea. Apart from a few of Roman ancestry the roads are narrow and were hurriedly made during the Second World War when this dreary marshland came extensively under the plough. Today its bright green vegetables feed millions and you are more likely to get stuck behind a tractor than a bus. The fields are big, the skies are enormous, the weather is elemental. And through this landscape, under vast drifting cloud castles run silver rivers upon which long, narrow boats crawl.

These narrow-boats were also refugees, for they had migrated from England's network of canals for cleaner, wider waterways teeming with wildlife and where ponderous locks are almost non-existent. These boats were now the homes of those who travelled within them and the Island was their harbour, the place they chugged forth from and returned to. The rivers linked with a network of other rivers and channels, most of them raised above the surrounding flat landscape, which encourages them to flow slowly towards the sea and so those who came to live on the boats on the Island had to assimilate in their minds the map of these waterways upon which they ventured forth as well as the map of the roads upon which they also travelled. It was confusing at first, but like everything else there it was just that things were different – this was mercifully a different, unique world.

Why would somebody seek out a different world, you may wonder? There must be as many reasons are there are people who are at odds with the way the world is. For myself the reason was I did not have peace, in fact I was just about at the end of my rope, decimated financially, emotionally and spiritually. I'd been divorced three times, lost two families, businesses and been made homeless twice. In the middle of all of this my second wife was extremely mentally unstable due to being raped as a child. She spent a large part of our time together either trying to kill me or herself. Happy days, eh? But at the time I begin this sorry tale I still had a roof over my head – and a job of sorts, but it paid badly and it wasn't going to last.

Clearly, I had to do something about the situation I was in. Suicide was an option I considered seriously on several occasions. After all, the experience of my life had taught me that living was a complete waste of time. I examined the situation logically. I'd tried so many things and failed at them. I'd never fitted in anywhere and I seemed to be destined to bear the consequences of other people's problems as well as my own. However, there was one drawback to the suicide option. I had a son and although I could see the logic and even the necessity of ending my life, I could not inflict that upon him. You see, I'd spent a fair amount of my working life in mental health and I understood how devastating the suicide of a parent is to their offspring. So, ending my life was not an option. Clearly, I had to find a different one.

As I've said, there have been other times in my life when I've faced disasters but, you know, something always happened to remedy my situation. As if in some kind of compensation, I'd long ago realised that the Universe would somehow take care of me. One time I was homeless and in very dire straights the Universe provided me with an empty monastery to live in – which at the time was exactly what I needed. Now in the knowledge of such benevolent cosmic intervention I felt that whatever I needed would be provided. Right on cue came the option of living on a narrowboat on the Island – something I'd never dreamed of considering. Now at the time, boats were one of the many things I knew absolutely nothing about, but as Abraham Lincoln once said 'ignorance is no obstacle to advancement'.

After a long search I found a boat for sale that was already there on the Island – which seemed like more cosmic intervention. She was twenty metres (70 feet) long - as long as such boats come and longer than most. An engineer friend advised me it was a good one – built in 1980 of good British steel – no recycled Ford Fiestas from Poland - and her beating heart was a 30 horsepower three-cylinder Lister diesel engine. Her name was Boudica – which struck me as a good omen for the Island was part of what had once been the warrior queen's Queendom. I sold my house, paid off the mortgage, made a very satisfying bonfire of all my bills and bank statements and I took a huge leap into the unknown. I did not know what my future might be. I only knew I could not go back to my old life. I had to trust the Universe would take care of me.

And so began my sixteen years living off grid – or probably as far off grid as someone could live in England at that time. It was a time in the wilderness – a time of learning, of rediscovering, connecting with countless things that have been lost to us. Now that I am returned from the Island, some years have passed and I've learned a great deal more to put with my insights from my time in the wilderness – after all that's what time in the wilderness is for.

Now as I write these words, the full magnitude of what has occurred over the past few years is beginning to be understood. People are waking up and discovering that things are not as they should be and they are confused and fearful. What this awakening may mean for the future we cannot yet imagine – however, I am of a positive mind set as the following pages will show and so I'm optimistic for the future.

Some of the answers to our situation I'm sure lie in the past, in what we have come to think of as the wilderness of humanity. I think that by somehow returning to the wilderness we may learn about just how much we've been swindled out of our birthright; we may begin to see where things went wrong and figure out a way to return to the place we deserve to be, now in the 21st century. This book is my contribution to that perspective. I'm going to try and recall that which I learned that may be useful and of interest to you the reader. I have no idea how this will turn out, but then as the man who wrote about the girl who went down a rabbit hole said; if you don't know where you're going…

There is a tide in the affairs of men which
taken at the flood leads on to fortune
Omitted all the voyages of their life,
Is bound in shallows and in miseries On
such a full sea we are now afloat, and we
must take the current when it serves, or lose
our ventures.

\-   William Shakespeare.

Burning Bridges

On the day I moved on to my boat there had certainly been a flood – which seemed like a particularly cruel cosmic joke at the beginning of my ventures. The road was flooded, even the connecting bridge to the Island was under three feet of water, the whole area was under water. The Island itself was completely cut off! I was stuck with a van load of my meagre possessions and three cats unable to even get to my boat wondering if the Universe was telling me something – but I couldn't go back. I had sold my house I had burnt my bridges. A long detour and a bumpy ride down a farm track got me closer to where my boat was moored, but the floods still prevented access. This did not seem fortunate at all - but the Universe was taking care of me. A friendly boat came chugging along, I put my possessions on the roof and we sailed around to where my boat was moored. Then it was a matter of transferring myself, my possessions and my three cats to Boudica via her roof hatch. It took a few days for the floods to subside and for access to the Island to be restored, but then I began my new life. Whether it would lead to fortune or not time would tell.

I had moved to the Island in the Spring of my 58th year – which wasn't by design as it happened, it just coincided with the end of the torture I'd suffered at the hands of solicitors and estate agents when I sold my house - but it did mean I would hopefully have some clement weather in which to adjust to my new life. To begin with I had to recover from the enormous degree of stress I had been under. This I knew would take time, but I had plenty of time – as much as I wanted - and I had plenty of practical things to do. However, I wasn't exactly alone – I had brought with me three cats – Sandy, Winston and Mad Moll. It was a shock to them at first, but they adjusted pretty quickly to boat life.

They say you are either a cat or a dog person and many of the boaters had dogs – in particular those who lived alone. Greyhounds and lurchers were the most popular as they are usually very placid and sleep a great deal. However, I'd come with three cats – which were the remains of the six I'd had with my last wife. Cats are self-sufficient, you don't have to pick up their poo or take them for walks in the pouring rain and they can be wonderful company, but they are still wild creatures and they do things their own way in their own time. Some cats are very cosmic – Winston was very connected with the universe. Mad Moll was endearing, but quite mad as her name suggests. Sandy was a big all white cat – he'd had an all-white brother named Julian who had been keen on raiding people's Goldfish ponds. Sadly, one night he never returned from a mission. I find dogs a little sycophantic and constantly demanding, but that's fine if you live on your own, but if I'm going to have company, I prefer it to be human – preferably female.

Everything was different but I found living in a steel box six-foot six wide by seventy feet long refreshingly secure. Some might imagine it to be a prison but actually it felt like a safe haven, something like a burrow under the ground that protects a vulnerable animal, sheltered and safe from predators - but in the case of a narrow boat this burrow could move, travel at my direction, when I wished it to. I didn't realise it at the time but I had inadvertently become a nomad - and we human beings have been nomadic for the vast majority of our existence. I was beginning a new life which was in essence a very old way of life albeit in a modern incarnation.

I didn't start out expecting to learn, but I learned so much. If I'm honest, I would have hoped to have used the opportunity to leave my previous life behind and forget all I'd known, but it didn't turn out that way. Going into the unknown is like entering the land of lost tomorrows – but then if the tomorrows you are going to lose are not the right tomorrows, then you'll need to find new ones. I had burnt my bridges, I could not go back even if I wanted to, I had entered an unknown wilderness and I'd hoped, I might eventually emerge from it into a new landscape, illuminated and full of promise.

It was strange at first, but exciting - a whole new adventure in a new place. I felt like a pioneer carving out a new destiny in a new land and indeed it had something of the flavour of the wild west about it. The area was sparsely populated then and the Island felt like a frontier settlement. This new land was a unique place – I don't think there is anywhere else like it in England. To begin with it's nothing like the canals, the canals are the remains of a water transport system that linked the industrial areas of this country with the ports, the mines, mills, factories and steel works – all the places that fuelled the industrial revolution. When the canals were dug they had to go through hills and across valleys. The engineers used existing rivers when they could, but they could only build this national transport network by utilising thousands of locks to take the water up and down the hills and dales. Locks are fascinating low-tech devices to watch, but in terms of travel they are slow and labour intensive.

As it happened, as soon as the canal network was carrying all the heavy bulkier things that needed to be moved around, someone invented the steam engine and then the railway which was faster than horses towing cumbersome barges. The canals began to decline especially after the Second World War (1939-1945) but in the 1960's they started to be used for leisure which led to a renaissance of the waterways. Boat builders began to make steel narrowboats which emulated the former commercial boats but were now used for holidays and could be hired out for a week or two. Boats such as the one I bought were former hire boats, but there are many new boats being built for private use these days – for holidays or for 'live-aboards'. Most are a standard six feet six inches wide that enables them to pass through the old locks but if you want more space, you can get a 'wide-beam' of ten or twelve feet in width – but they cannot go through most locks so their use is limited – at least if you want to travel. Increasingly people are choosing to live on these boats due to the cost and shortage of housing, however boat life has its pros and cons. I think it's fair to say most people would not choose to live on a boat if they had the option, but there are those like me who were desperate to escape the madness and live an alternative lifestyle, closer to nature.

The canals were definitely not for me, as the best of them get horrendously crowded in Summer and subject to 'lock rage' by impatient holiday boaters. I was fortunate that the system of waterways I had found myself on were not canals at all but rivers and drainage channels created over hundreds of years to drain the Fens. Once this area had been an inland sea that had become a vast marshland full of tangled forests and swamps. The few people that had lived there were those who had been driven from the mainland by poverty or villainy, they survived on a few scattered islands by hunting wildfowl, fish and in particular eels. They were often plagued by diseases like malaria, their only dubious compensation being opium poppies. Now drained, this area teemed with wildlife, the waterways flowed out to the sea - albeit slowly, it was not dead and stagnant like some of the canal system is.

This new world I found myself in was certainly an alternative one and I had much to learn, but as I faced this new future, I didn't know that my adventure would take me back to a distant time that is in a sense still with us, under the surface of our modern lives and the real learning, the real adventure was the buried treasure I would discover there. Islands and treasure, eh? It sounds like there ought to be pirates – and there were, but not the kind with parrots on their shoulders - these were people who were living outside the normal way of life in the 21st century. Some were wild, crazy even - but I never met any that were violent. These were people who had either chosen or been driven away from the madness of the modern world. They were all individuals, all very different yet they had found this unique water world where they were relatively free to be themselves, to live how they wanted, to be as sociable or unsociable as they chose. Those pirates taught me a great deal also. There was a kind of camaraderie I suppose. Help was always available and nobody was interested in what gadgets or possessions you had or how expensive your boat was or the car you drove or how much money you might have. We were simply people 'all in the same boat' as it were.

Are you aware, there's another side of life, another side of life out there?

Far off away is the other side of life yet the other side of life is here

Have you time to spare? Can I take you there?

Could you get wise to another side of life, another side of life out there?

Open your eyes to another side of life, another side of life we could share

Have you time to spare? Can I take you there?

Another Side Of Life - Les Richards

Living on the Island was different in almost every way for me. For one thing I'd always owned my own house, I'd never rented a place to live and here I was at the mercy of the owner of the Island who was effectively renting me a mooring. At least I owned my boat completely and as it happened the owner was by no means a tyrant – in fact he basically let us boaters get on with our lives and didn't bother us at all, so far from feeling insecure I had the freedom to leave whenever I wanted which was strangely empowering. I'd never expected this bonus and it was the first of many things that seemed to turn my perceptions around and allowed me to reassess my attitude to life – and there were many such lessons to be learned.

To begin with, a really big thing I had to learn was how to use my boat. 'Bou' as everyone called her was very long – there were only two other 70 footers on the Island and I was a complete novice. I had no experience of boats whatsoever, I can't even swim. Manoeuvring this huge thing out onto the main river seemed almost impossible at first, but I had plenty of help and plenty of advice. Even so, my mouth was dry as I grasped the tiller and ventured forth for the first couple of dozen times, but with much practice, I mastered the process. I even made the time-honoured mistake of trying to leave with the Electric cable still plugged in!

In time I learned to go through a set routine when preparing to leave and a reverse routine when coming back to moor up. I learned to lay out the long mooring ropes correctly so I could reach them without falling in the river and to get everything handy so I could reach things without leaving the tiller. If only I could have learned how to set forth on the journey of my own life so easily!

Bou's handling was very poor and although a 30 horse power three-cylinder Lister diesel engine might sound powerful it was not very effective at pushing sixteen tons of sluggish steel along. Good enough I supposed for going in straight lines along canals but not enough for life on the rivers where the wind was often a big problem to contend with. Speed is not something you get a narrow boat for, but Bou would never have been any use for towing water skiers! Her usual speed without the noise and vibration becoming intolerable was what I would imagine to be a fast-walking pace – which doesn't sound much but believe me when you want to slow down or stop you have the momentum of an oil tanker to consider. How many times in my past had I kept on going when I should have stopped or at least changed my direction?

Learning to control an unwieldy narrow boat was frightening at first but there was never any lack of advice (often contradictory) from my fellow islanders. Going forwards is pretty straightforward (if you'll excuse the pun) but it takes time to get used to the length and allow for the things you can't see. From the tiller the entire boat looks rather like a narrowing, pointed cone in front, but there is so much you can't see to consider.

It doesn't help that the roof is covered with solar panels, bicycles, boat hooks, long poles and other paraphernalia. Steering by tiller means you turn it to the left to turn right and vice versa. I mastered that easily enough but stopping is a question of reducing the power to the propeller, perhaps even reversing the drive but everything happens so slowly, every action has a delayed reaction. To go backwards is a mind-boggling process that flies in the face of all logic. I'm reminded that attempting to reverse or change the course of my life had seemed equally impossible.

The technique is practically unexplainable but I'll try. From a dead stop you can put the boat into reverse gear and it will go backwards, but the tiller has almost no effect – that's because there is no water being thrust against the rudder – which is *behind* the prop, the water is being directed forwards to the front which is no good from a steering point of view. The only way to change the boat's rearward direction is to put the rudder over about 45 degrees and put the engine in *forward* gear. It sounds crazy, but by doing this the prop blast pushes the stern to the left or right. Once the stern is in the desired direction you can reverse again.

The rule to remember is 'no gear, no steer' – which means if the gearbox is in neutral the propeller is idle. Eventually, I got so good at this that when I returned and reversed into my mooring people would come out to watch and marvel at my prowess. It's good for your confidence to be the focus of admiration but you absolutely dare not get it wrong. Just as in life when you make a mistake the spectators will not be impressed.

The other manoeuvre is turning the boat in a complete circle – providing the river is wide enough you can put the bow into the bank and swing the back around with the engine and rudder hard over. It looks impressive, but you have to be sure of the length of the boat.

Learning to control my boat made me realise that I had not been in control of my life – I'd been blown and dragged along by capricious winds and dangerous currents and my ability to stop, start, turn and steer was almost negligible. No wonder I had collided with so many obstacles and done myself so much damage, but why had I been such a poor Captain of my own life, why hadn't I been capable of steering myself?

I was born in 1948 just three years after the Second World War in a village that was then about 20 miles from London. I often woke in the mornings to the sound of chickens and distant machine gun fire – these were comforting sounds to me. The chickens were in the garden – it was very common then for people to keep them – I was not aware of what the machine gun fire represented, but it came from the Royal Powder Mills at Waltham Abbey where they made explosives and ammunition which was a long way away - the world then was a much quieter place.

It was a world where if you sat on the roadside it took most of the day to fill a page of car numbers and on Sunday afternoons the family would walk about 2 miles to sit in the grass beside what was then known as the Arterial Road to watch cars pass by. I had one sister who was considerably older than me so I was essentially an only child. My parents were of an age and class that had bestowed upon them a very rudimentary education and worse still a lack of will or interest to broaden their own intellectual horizons, yet for some reason my mind was filled with an insatiable desire for knowledge.

Thus, I was a very lonely child who found little in common with the limited number of my peers I had contact with. I naturally felt isolated in a family that didn't know how to show or express love, showed little appetite for life, or appreciation for the wonders of the world. There were no books to speak of, nothing to read but a dull newspaper - but there was the radio.

In the UK of the early 1950's before television became widely available there was only the radio (then called wireless because I assume the set plugged into the mains electricity rather than being attached to an 'accumulator' – battery). Scanning a radio dial brought forth a tantalising wealth of incomprehensible foreign stations so there was only the state broadcaster - the BBC in English.

There were then three channels – 'The Home Service' which was practically all news, current affairs and lectures that were aimed at the middle and upper classes, the 'Third Programme' was almost exclusively classical music and lastly for the plebs - the working class there was the 'Light Programme' – which during the day was aimed mostly at housewives. It offered some music – mostly played by 'in house' bands and orchestras – actual records were rarely heard - but there was a fair amount of comedy content which exercised the imagination somewhat because you could only hear it not see it.

Consequently, this limited window on the world beyond was pretty much all I was exposed to in my early years. It was an intellectual wilderness that I hungered to escape from. My questing mind turned inwards, finding stimulation and connection with the natural world. I sought solace outside, in the woods and country lanes and footpaths that I explored. I stayed out as long as I could, no threat could keep me from wandering.

To be free of the stifling, oppressive and fearful atmosphere of my home was my salvation, usually alone feeling the companionship of the wild places, listening to messages that came on the wind in the trees, the ever-changing skies – these were my real friends. 'Why' is a big question – as a child I asked it constantly as some children do. I continually asked 'why' throughout my life and although I found many answers I still ask 'why'. After all, if you don't ask you won't get an answer, but there are so many 'whys' that are not answered.

How far back can you remember? I wonder what your earliest memory is? My earliest memory is of sitting in my push chair at maybe two years old in a busy place with crowds of people all around me and above me was the most wonderful flawless blue sky. I remember I could not understand why all these people who were much taller than me and therefore closer to the sky were ignoring it completely.

As I grew up I realised that most of my fellow human beings took very little notice of the world around them yet I still did. In fact, I found myself striving to make an ever-greater connection with the Universe. Of course this tended to isolate me from everyone else. However, I came across the words of writers and poets who clearly had the same experiences – and that made me feel less of a loner. This was one I heard as a child at primary school…

Glad that I live am I that the sky is blue
Glad for the country lanes and the fall of dew
After the sun the rain, after the rain the sun
This is the way of life 'till the work be done

All that we need to do, be we low or high
Is to see that we grow nearer to the sky
After the sun the rain, after the rain the sun This
is the way of life 'till the work be done

-   Lizette W Reese 1856-1935 American poet and teacher

The more I came across these words of connection I wondered why most people didn't feel the connection and why I did feel it? Was it some past memory that most people were too busy to remember? The more I've learned the more I believe this was the case. This connection to the Universe is to me a spiritual connection and for me the Universe and God are one and same. To ignore this is to reject our true nature, to deny ourselves our complete humanity. It took me a lifetime to accept that I was different from most people in that I always felt half in this world and half outside it connected to the Universe beyond. It was lonely to be that way, to not fit in, but I found beautiful and profound compensations.

When I was in primary school the teacher read to the class a story called 'The Little Grey Men' by an author named simply 'BB'. This was a tale about three gnomes – the last left in England who lived beside a stream and decided to build a boat and travel upstream to search for their long-lost brother. It's an Odyssey type of story and it attracted me so strongly that I think it subconsciously guided me to living on the river so many years later. The author had written many books on fishing and wildlife as well as children's books and I instinctively understood that he connected with the natural world the same as I did. This was a great comfort to me as a lonely isolated child. Each one of his books had at the beginning a quote which I now have framed on my living room wall.

The wonder of the world, the beauty and the power,
The shapes of things, their colours, lights and shades These I
saw,
Look ye also while life lasts

-      Text from an old Cumbrian gravestone prefacing all BB's books.

I've always loved to read. In fact, the Secondary school I went to was so bad I used to skip lessons and go to my local library to get an education. Libraries are wonderful places although these days they seem to be less contaminated by actual books. However, now we do have the most amazing library in history – the Internet - and everything you ever wanted to know can be found therein. I was born with a thirst for knowledge but I soon found out that most of those around me had little interest in learning.

Even today when there is so much knowledge freely available a great many people seem stuck in some self-imposed intellectual desert. They play on-line games instead of enjoying the incredible range of fascinating insights they could get from countless YouTube videos about every subject imaginable. Many people can't seem to tear themselves away from mindless TV soap operas. Consequently, they believe only what they are told by government propaganda, their perceptions are shaped by advertising and so they have not broadened their minds or their horizons – quite the opposite it seems.

Book sales are declining, fewer people bother to read and even fewer write, yet a book can contain the most priceless treasures, a book can motivate, educate, liberate, even change your life, a book can take you into the mind of someone from another country in another time. People rarely listen to stories told orally – which is tragic when you learn that for thousands of years before printing was invented storytelling was the only way knowledge was passed on. There were even professional storytellers who used to travel around performing stories to people in the inns of settlements and villages, stories that sometimes took weeks to tell. There was also vital information contained within folk tales - stories for children mostly, but within them crucial knowledge was passed down through generations by archetypal imagery and analogies that planted the necessary wisdom directly into their eager, receptive minds.

The two oldest stories known were passed on this way. The *Iliad* about the ancient city of Troy and the *Odyssey* about Jason and Argonauts are both mythical stories about events that contain profound truths and vital information. In fact, the themes in these two stories are repeated again and again in all our stories, novels, dramas and movie scripts. Now I was living my own Odyssey and I would learn so much from my own personal story.

The individual has always had to struggle to keep from being overwhelmed by the tribe.
To be your own man is a hard business – if you try it you will be lonely often and sometimes frightened, but no price is too high to pay for the privilege of owning yourself

-    Kipling

How right Mr. Kipling was, yet why do many people hide their individuality and are seemingly content to run with the herd? After all there are billions of people and none of them are the same – they're all different – yet there appears to be an almost unanimous desire to conform. Conformity is a kind of cowardice, a fear of showing and exploring your own uniqueness. Why is this when we certainly were not herd animals in the distant past? If anything, we were hunter-gatherers or parasitic predators upon the wild herds. It was our ability to exploit this difference that made us what we were. If history teaches us anything it's that it was the individuals who changed things, some for the better, some for the worst.

I read someplace that a high percentage of people are genetically linked to Ghenkis Khan. Clearly, he must have made a big difference to the human race. But there would not have been an Einstein, a Bhuda or a Jesus, a Lao Tsu or a Hitler, or a Stalin unless these people were not afraid to use their individuality. It's the individual thinkers who make things happen, who change things. If that were not the case, we'd still be little furry animals scurrying between the feet of dinosaurs instead of sophisticated beings who can journey to other worlds. Is everything the consequence of random throws of the evolutionary dice – or is it as it seems to me that there is some great cosmic plan behind it all? Science and God seem reluctant to talk to each other, yet millions of people talk to the Universe all the time. I know, I'm one of them.

The steam of knowledge is heading towards a non-mechanical reality,
The universe begins to look more like a great thought than a great machine.

-    Sir James Jeans 1877-1946 English Physicist

When I was in the process of changing my life, I was surprised that almost everyone who had known I was selling up everything and going to live on a boat was extremely supportive, envious even. Many of them said it had long been their dream to do so – but of course they didn't or couldn't do it themselves. Perhaps that was why they applauded my adventure. For me it was not just a matter of choice it was a realisation that I could not carry on as I was. I'd made enough mistakes and lived through enough disasters to goad me into action and my decision to take this course was a practical one even though I'm sure some people thought it was crazy to opt out of 'normal' life.

Thinking back, I see now that it was what I'd always wanted but had never really admitted to myself. After all I'd never fitted in, never felt comfortable and never really succeeded in much for very long. Everything that had happened to me was telling me to change my life – I just didn't know how until the right time and circumstances arrived.

There was this one brief moment when I finally made up my mind to definitely go ahead. I was a passenger in a car and we crossed over a river and just for a second, I glimpsed a narrow boat chugging, a man standing on the stern holding the tiller, the sunlight silvering the water, going somewhere, a man steering his own course. I not only thought that I could do that myself – I actually wanted to do that. It was an image that flashed into my mind - yet it was enough to convince me of my path. Was it a message from the Universe perhaps? Why was that boat passing along that river at that exact moment I was passing across it? Things like that happen, call them omens, portents, revelations if you like – but they are messages we should not ignore. I think that in the past we were more closely attuned to recognizing such messages from the Universe.

In these modern times we've forgotten how to read the signs that may be all around us. We think we are beyond such things; we regard them as outdated - as cranky superstitions, but they surely happen and there must be a reason they do. Carl Jung the famous Austrian psychologist studied these messages and he wondered if they were merely coincidences, seemingly random events that form patterns but sometimes appear to have profound consequences? He described them as 'meaningful coincidences that cannot be explained by cause and effect'. He hypothesised that these occur when a person's individual, personal consciousness aligns with the Collective Consciousness – which creates a meaningful connection between inner and outer experiences.

I think we ignore these things to our detriment. We are not so advanced and sophisticated as we sometimes fool ourselves into believing. I think we've been extremely foolish to ignore and forget the common knowledge we once used to share. Perhaps if we can recapture some of what has been lost we might learn from it. Knowledge and wisdom are not things to be superseded and replaced by new concepts – they exist to be built upon and expanded. We are not as smart as we think we are, in fact I believe in many ways we've become dumber, less articulate and more ignorant than we used to be – and that's certainly not progress – it's a tragedy.

We should have the humility and honesty to own up to our ignorance. We should open the doors to our past, not shut them. That maybe a hard thing to admit but we should be honest about it. We are so often fearful, lost, confused and overwhelmed by life. It can take so much courage to be honest with yourself - I'm not sure why that is exactly. Maybe it's because we're trapped into conforming with everyone else. For me it was courage mixed with desperation I think, but having chosen my destiny I had to learn the ways of my new life. Somehow, I had the faith to try.

So here I was in the latter part of the 20th Century, an ageing dropout, living as near as I could to being a nomad from a river village, living in an alternative world that contained echoes of the long distant past and gradually learning how to readjust my life. I was learning from the new experiences how I could steer and control my own life. It's something of a tradition for those who search for answers, knowledge and wisdom to go off into the wild, empty places. It's there far away from civilization that the great mysteries are revealed to the uninitiated, isn't it? Here in these pages, I will attempt to pass on some of what I discovered on my journeying, here are some insights from my exile in an English wilderness. I sincerely hope they will be of use to you. Maybe they will at least cause you to think, to question, to challenge your own perceptions of your life, the world you inhabit, the past and the future.

I'm not an academic, I'm not an expert on anything so you might not regard my reflections as having any value – but that would be a grave mistake in my opinion. One of the problems I've so often come across is that people trust the words of experts and ignore the testimony and experience of people who have lived real lives in the real world.

We have teachers who went to school then to college, university perhaps and then teacher training establishments. Consequently, they know little or nothing about real people in real life. What's worse is that some of these so-called experts will become lecturers who teach the teachers – that is they'll pass on their own warped view of the world – which usually consists of the bizarre political theories of over-privileged 'intellectuals' who also had no experience of the real world.

Now we have engineers who learned engineering from a computer and not from wielding a spanner. We have Physicians who are trained by the pharmaceutical industry and not by doctors with a lifetime of experience. We have politicians who emerge from exclusive elite schools and pass straight into governments without ever running a business or working in a paid job. We even have mechanics who know only how to plug a diagnostic computer application into your car and know little about the idiosyncrasies of the internal combustion engine.

So, now we have experts who know more and more about less and less. Few people bother to listen to the testimonies of real people who have had real lives and their experiences are not incorporated into the wealth of knowledge we might otherwise inherit. The wisdom of our elders is ignored, the skills perfected by lifetimes of craftsmen and women are considered quaint but obsolete. The river of knowledge that irrigates our lives is now polluted, clogged with bullshit and toxic ideas. Consequently, the world is up shit creek without a paddle.

In a time of universal deceit - telling the truth is a revolutionary act

- George Orwell

Adjustments

The first negative aspect of living on the water I experienced was being bitten by monster mosquitoes which had thrived due to the flooding – but this only happened at the beginning of my time on the Island. The second thing I found something of a challenge were the toilets. There are basically two alternatives. Some boats have built in poo tanks into which all the excrement and waste water goes. These tanks (they are usually hidden beneath the floor level often under the seating) don't take long to fill up especially if you live aboard permanently. That means they have to be pumped out which is a most unpleasant and very smelly job.

The other problem was that there were very few 'pump outs' on the system and you might spend a day getting to one only to find it out of order. These tanks were usually taken out leaving more precious space for other things. Most boaters use the second alternative – a cassette toilet. This is a plastic box with the detachable top half loosely resembling a normal toilet seat which contains a built-in tank that holds a water and a blue chemical solution which can be sealed off by simply sliding a lever enabling you to detach the bottom portion of the toilet (the cassette) to take it away and empty it in the place provided. This is usually a big underground tank which is sucked out maybe once a month by a smelly bloke in a smelly tanker lorry.

There was on the Island, close by the rubbish bins and the mailboxes, an attractive structure built in the fashion of a wishing well. However, it was certainly not a place to throw coins and wish – it was the place where the boaters emptied their cassette toilets. They would need emptying maybe once a week into the tank beneath the wishing well. This was a short but unpleasant job and only moderately smelly, but it was often the case that a fellow boater would wander by while you were emptying your toilet and washing it clean. It was surprisingly natural to engage in a lengthy conversation while doing so. The proximity of another person to the smell of one's excrement was a great leveller. Modern living has turned what was once a perfectly ordinary natural function to become a taboo subject for discussion but on the Island such pretensions were swept away by the refreshing wind of reality.

One stormy night when I had not been living on my boat for that long I had a scary experience. I awoke to find my world had slipped into an alarming angle. Was I dreaming? No. Groggily I realised that the water level had risen and so had the boat. It was pitch black, the wind howling and three-o-clock in the morning. Clearly, I had to sort this problem out now and on my own. Elemental stuff. Outside on the jetty I struggled with a torch. The main rope was tied on the central mooring lug on the roof. The rope was pulling about 16 tons of steel over to one side. It was a miracle it hadn't snapped or pulled the fixings out of the wooden jetty. I understood that it was going to be difficult enough to untie the knot, when the rope was released there would be a moment of extreme danger.

I was alone, I had to do this right. By the light of the torch, I managed to ease the knot – a reef knot – about the only one I can tie as it happens, but probably the most useful as a reef knot will almost never undo on its own, its symmetry is security, but once that pattern is loosened it will come apart easily. Slowly I eased the knot, the rope was like a bowstring, I had to keep my fingers well away when it released, otherwise I could have lost them. There was no chance of rousing anyone to get me to A & E at that time of night either. I could have been thrown into the river, crushed between the hull and the jetty. I could have drowned, as I couldn't even float let alone swim, but there was no time to think of such things, this was the time for cool, calm action.

Slowly, I got the knot loose and with a groan the boat rolled back on to an even keel. I stood back relieved. I'd done it. Phew. I checked the bow and stern ropes. They were OK. I vowed that I would buy some of those steel rings that ride up and down the mooring poles as the water level fluctuates so this situation wouldn't happen again. I went back to bed, lesson learned, my confidence enhanced. There was a crisis and I had sorted it out. Survival. Elemental.

Was it also an analogy I wondered? My life had been distorted, out of level, unstable. I had made a choice, I had changed my life and as the emergency illustrated, I had stabilised it through purely my own efforts. This was a big lesson for me to learn because hitherto my life had consisted of one crisis after another and I had been constantly overwhelmed by them. I was a helpless piece of flotsam swept along by merciless currents and I had been powerless to direct my own course, but now after abandoning the poisonous world I had been living in I had changed my course. I was no longer in the wrong place cut off from my connection to the Universe. I was on the right track now; I fitted this new life and it in turn fitted me. There were no more storms for me to be swept away by. I was my own Captain; I steered my own ship aided by the compass of my connection with the Universe to guide me.

Why had it taken me so long to begin to take control of my own life? I can see now there were many reasons but the main one was I lacked the confidence to do so. Even so, there had been times when I had been the beneficiary of what I would know as universal intervention. I had actually been given miracles in my life that should have made me wake up, but although I certainly valued those intervals of salvation it took a long time and lots more chaos before I found my courage, to leave the world that was so toxic to me and the life that was constantly trying to destroy me.

Everything that happens to us, properly understood, leads us back to ourselves

-    C.G. Jung

My boat was a rather boring Oxford blue all over which I resolved to change as soon as I could. Now that I'd found another world where I could sail my own ship it seemed important that it should be painted in my choice of colours. This would help me assert it was mine alone - much like a knight's heraldry. This somewhat ostentatious concept was new to me as all the years I'd driven a car I'd never wanted it to stand out in any way and I'd been most reluctant to invite attention. From my fellow islanders I learnt that if you wanted to paint your boat you realistically had a brief window after the Winter before the willow fluff falls. The willow trees were everywhere, they grow quickly and self-replicate either by allowing their branches to fall and take root, or in the late Spring they send out billions of seeds in the willow fluff. These white tufts fall like snow covering the surface of the water and just about everything else so if you're going to paint anything you have to get it done before the fluff comes.

I experimented with some colour schemes on photoshop and decided to forego the usual dark greens which seemed to be popular and go for something more spectacular. I didn't see my boat as a facsimile canal boat, I didn't share the false romanticism of what must have been a terribly gruelling life of poverty for the people who lived and worked on the canals. I felt more like a gypsy who would have had a painted caravan, a free spirit rather than a commercial slave. I did not wish to mimic the industrial past, I wanted to create an alternative present and so my boat became resplendent with big red panels bordered with yellow coach lines against dark blue beneath a light blue roof. I wanted her to be unique, celebrated, recognized.

There was no time to waste and after extensive rubbing down with an angle grinder and sanding discs painting was a pleasant and rewarding job, covering the boat first with red oxide, then two grey undercoats followed by two coats with bright colour, the cuckoo serenading my efforts and reminding me to get on with the job before the willow fluff descended. Later I would paint some Celtic artwork on the sides and the name Boudica upon her bows and stern, but I achieved the basic re-paint just before the willow fluff began to cascade down.

There was also a great deal that needed to be changed inside the boat. This would take time and would need to happen organically, for I needed to see what changes would suit me – but I had all the time I wanted. Some days I woke up and worked on the boat, some days I didn't, but I had the luxury of time. No clock to watch, no conversation to cut short because I had to be somewhere else. I had time for people and to do things with them if they needed a hand moving a boat or simply wanted company. Time for people is a wonderful luxury that most people don't have any more, but now I did. Time - which is in such short supply in the outer world - was flexibly in abundance there on the Island, time to talk to people, time to look at the water, the sky, time to simply be. That work that you planned to do could wait until tomorrow if a friend visited, or the river called. You could eat when you were hungry, sleep when you were tired and not when the clock ordered.

Natural sleep is another great liberation I began to experience – to get up in the night to write maybe, or have an afternoon nap – which lowers your mind to a beautiful level of consciousness. Consciousness itself became something different, reality became realer, simply breathing was easier and my mind could be free to dwell on things banal or eternal. We are meant to wake slowly, indulge in revelry, collect our thoughts until we are ready to face the day. We are not meant to be torn from our dreams by alarms as if we are fighter pilots tasked with a dangerous mission.

Before the Industrial Revolution it was common for people to wake halfway through the night and visit neighbours – especially if there was good moonlight. Of course, they would have retired much earlier than we do today as they didn't have the benefit of good artificial lighting. Natural sleep is another of those things that has been taken from us by the way we've been conditioned to live. Few people now get enough sleep and so they keep awake by drinking gallons of coffee. I read that samples taken from the Atlantic Ocean off the coast of the USA show huge amounts of caffeine in the water. More evidence that the world is crazy. I was fortunate to rediscover natural sleep and by doing so I found another connection with our past.

It took a long time (years in fact) to get the inside of my boat how I wanted it. It was a gradual process not least because I did most of it myself. There were some things that had to remain where they were – like the kitchen. I moved the bedroom from the back of the boat to the front and made a new area for my compact recording studio. The lounge had two long seats one each side which were great for relaxing or even sleeping on. The wood burning range was between the lounge and the kitchen.

Next, I put in a useful work top area which could be used to eat or work at. There was lots of storage underneath. Opposite there were narrow cupboards that stored two of my guitars. Next the shower and toilet, then the new bedroom. Things changed a little over the sixteen years I lived there but it was very cosy and functional. The great thing about it was that it was mine – it belonged to no one else. I ultimately had it my way – after all I was Captain of my own ship.

The man who follows the crowd will usually get no further than the crowd. The man who walks alone is likely to find himself in places no one has ever been

- Alan Ashley-Pitt

As time passed, my connection to my new home grew and the new world I was living in – and the old world where I had lived my whole life receded. It was still a place I visited now and then – a shopping trip perhaps - but even that became a quick dash into the nearest town early in the morning before the mass of people came out, then quickly back to the Island usually before 9 a.m. so that the whole day was mine. I would spend my time in the early days working on the interior of the boat, slowly getting things how they suited me.

There is an important factor you must take into consideration when you change things around in a boat – that is balance. Because it floats on the water there is no permanent horizontal and so it follows that there is also no permanent vertical. Every boat has ballast to keep it at the best level in the water. The ballast usually consists of lots of heavy paving slabs under the floor - but when you add in heavy things like a big cast iron stove the boat goes over to the side it's on. That means you have to compensate by adding things to the other side to balance it out. This all takes time of course but you get there eventually. There is also extra movable ballast under the front deck and at the stern in the engine bay. A full tank of water makes a big difference as it pushes the bow down in the water – but hey - at least you can tell when the tank needs filling.

I was also learning to balance myself – my own life and just like a boat there are heavy objects we carry around that weigh you down or skew your angle on things. Getting all that to balance takes a lot of time – but you have to do it if you're going to travel in equilibrium.

Making any change in your life is not an easy thing to do. It's risky to leave behind what you know even if that is not such a good place to be. People endure bad marriages for years before they leave them or are forced to go. How many people endure working in jobs they despise but stay because they fear the unknown? How is it we've come to believe that the unknown is inevitably going to be bad? Is this what we were forced to believe when we abandoned our old nomadic ways?

The old maps had 'Here be dragons' written on the unexplored areas but a few brave people still set sail for undiscovered lands. Why is it that most of us are too damned chicken to change our lives?

What is life? For most people it's growing up, getting an education, finding a job and a home – and someone to share it with, but to achieve our aims can cost us dearly. Even if we are fortunate enough to get a good start, a good education, a worthwhile career and eventually find the perfect partner to share it all we are faced with a lifetime of doing what we don't really want to be doing, in places we would rather not be, spending almost all the wealth we create to just keep ourselves on the hamster wheel with a roof over our heads, food and clothes, heat and power, transport, communication and a few consumer goodies, but if all that is enough for you then that's cool. It was never what I wanted, although to be honest I didn't know what I really wanted – but I did know what I didn't want and perhaps that's a good place to begin any journey into unknown territory.

You see, I'd never fitted in anywhere, but when I went to live on the Island for the first time in my life, I found that I did fit in. I still had a great deal to learn, but as I learned, most of what I discovered were things that we humans had somehow forgotten and thus I began to find my true self at long last. I eventually came to understand that I'd been living in a world where I did not belong – the world I belonged to was a place where everything is connected to the greater Universe and today's world has been torn away from that original 'Garden of Eden'. The Island I'd found was a small remaining piece of the Garden – a direct equivalent of the river villages that the Neolithic people inhabited in this same area. How miraculous is that?

Perhaps it's because we've been conditioned to settle in one place since the invention of agriculture some ten thousand years ago and we've been made to believe that to move elsewhere is dangerous. Yet with the discovery of the 'New World' of America by European explorers, courageous people migrated to find a better life, sometimes their motivation was religious persecution, sometimes to seek the promise of a better life free of the class systems of European countries.

Millions of Irish people fled to America because of famine caused by a disease called potato blight – which is ironic when you consider the potato came from the Americas in the first place. The Scots went because they were evicted by wealthy landowners, people from Africa went as slaves and had no choice in the matter. Millions left the old world with little more than their dreams to sustain them, they crossed the vast continent in wagons looking for a new life, a new start. They were people who had nothing to lose but their oppression and their poverty and many of them perished in the process, their dreams and hopes unfulfilled – but at least they tried and many of them succeeded, built new lives and founded a new nation that became the most powerful in the world.

Whatever their motivation was, those courageous people changed their circumstances and many found the freedom and success that would have been impossible had they stayed behind. Those people instinctively knew that they needed to find a new life and the way to find it was to move to new places – just like the nomadic peoples of the past they understood that when the pastures are depleted, eaten bare by the migrating herds, they naturally move onward to where the grass is greener and fresher, they followed the seasonal cycles.

I had not been much of a traveller myself, I'd lived mostly in the County I was born in, although I did move to Suffolk with my third wife and that was starting a new life in a way, for it was a big thing for me to leave the area I had always known, but I was so glad that I did it. I once knew many young people who had left former Communist countries and worked their way across Europe learning new languages, new skills seeking a better life. They humbled me in that I had not had the courage to change my own life for the better, I had remained in a life that continually tried to destroy me, but their courage rubbed off and when the time and opportunity came my way I made the move. I'd run out of choices and to buy a boat and live on it in a new world was the only practical option I had. It was time to take some action, take some control over my life. My boat was the equivalent of a covered wagon, the means of carrying me through an unexplored new world. I was not without fear and just like those millions of other migrants I was burning my bridges, risking everything, but the time had come for me – it was time to go.

When the sun goes down and the lights come on
Ten thousand lonely jewels on a black velvet tapestry
And you feel the call in the traffic flow reaching out
across the city and somehow you know

And you feel the beat of a vacant heart calling out to you and somehow you know

*That it makes no sense to do nothing at all, better take a
chance – yes, it's time to go*

*Don't you know, this is the time to go, don't you know this is
the time to go*

*Take a crowded train, take a camel ride, fly an antique plane,
take a magic carpet ride*
*Pack an empty bag with an open mind, with the moon on your
shoulder leave it all behind*
*Don't you know, this is the time to go, don't you know this is
the time to go*

*There's an empty house with a golden key down a long
winding road that leads to the sea*
When the sun comes up and it's a brand new day
With the wind in your hair you'll be sailing away
*Don't you know, this is the time to go, don't you know this is
the time to go*

Time to Go – Les Richards

The Essentials

Just like those early travellers I couldn't take everything along on my journey. I had to dispose of what was not needed, I had to leave a great deal of my stuff behind. Everybody has stuff, everywhere – in the loft, in the garage, in the shed maybe. You know the stuff I mean, the things you've done with and can't be bothered to throw away - just in case you might need it. The stuff that fills our homes, our cupboards – the things we don't need, we don't use, but seem incapable of disposing of; clothes, furniture, books, toys, CD's, things we have replaced, outgrown, rejected, things that are obsolete - and things are becoming obsolete at an ever-increasing rate. We live in a world that produces things that are designed to become obsolete and so we consign them to the unused places in our homes where they contribute nothing to our lives but clog the space and gather dust. These things not only anchor us to the past, they constrain the development of our future and thinking about it, the word stuff is most appropriate because these things clog up the cosmic wheels and impede our development and our future possibilities.

When a parent dies their house has to be cleared. Not only does it contain a lifetime's accumulation of stuff, it's often the repository of all the stuff the other family members chose to store or dump there. You would not believe how much stuff there is; furniture that will never be used, tools, pots, pans, ornaments, clothes, papers, magazines – my God! You've never seen so much stuff and now it has to be sorted through and got rid of. This is usually a most unwelcome legacy to those who are forced to inherit it. Although the process of getting rid of the stuff irked me greatly, I do have sympathy. I've had to do this myself of course and I know how the emotional bond of stuff holds us. I've assisted several other people in this task – I guess it comes with age. People die and their stuff must go and where does it go? To the auctions, the charity shops, then it might get recycled, but most of it usually ends up in a hole in the ground. This is a tragic waste - this is an insane way to live and an appalling use of the resources of our planet.

Living on a boat, a tube six-feet-six wide by seventy feet long is like living in a corridor somebody once said to me - but corridors are for passing through, not living in. There is no space on the boat for anything but the essentials and perhaps a few treasured possessions. I was told when I embarked on my semi-nomadic existence that if I didn't use something for six months then I didn't need it. It was good advice. When I came to the boat, I thought I'd whittled my possessions down to a bare minimum. How wrong I was - I was still throwing things away for the next couple of years.

Eventually, I'd paired everything down to the essentials. I had practically no furniture as it was all built into the boat. I had only the clothes I actually needed, but I still regularly disposed of stuff. Books, unwanted clothes and DVDs from the charity shop went back there when I'd done with them, anything that could be burned went on the stove towards heating and cooking. I didn't buy what I didn't need.

This was not an easy process, but it gets easier the more you do it. Photographs are probably the hardest thing to purge from your life, but by going through them you come to realise they are just images of memories from the past – they tie us to the past and impede our vision of the future. Our memories belong in our minds not in an album. At least when I go, there will be very little stuff for my remaining family to deal with - probably one car trip to the charity shop should take care of it. I used to favour the idea of a Viking funeral - which would clear everything in one go, but I imagined the burned-out hull of my boat might be a hazard to navigation.

I came to learn that the most negative aspect of stuff is that it prevents us from accessing what comes freely to us from the Universe, from nature, from our fellow travellers, our companions. When I discovered this fact, I was astounded. I cannot even begin to describe to you the value of the unseen, immaterial treasure that came to me for free when I got rid of the stuff. I guess you can only find this out for yourself. Anyway, it was a revelation - I finally understood that the stuff prevents us from our true connection with the Universe and that gave me another revelation – the need to have stuff is denying us our true human heritage – our connection with the Universe.

On the Island I was taken back to a different time, when we had more basic needs. The use of fire was of course a profound development in our history, one that had only a beneficial impact as far as I can see. One of the many stupid questions I used to get asked was: isn't it cold living on a boat? Well of course if you don't light the stove it will be cold just the same as if you didn't switch on the central heating in a house. However, the boat stove is much more than heat - it is an essential component of life – heat, hot water and cooking.

At the very least, a boat would have a small cast iron stove upon which a kettle simmered or a stew steamed. The best of these life sustaining stoves was the Squirrel – recognizable by a representation of a squirrel cast in the iron. It's a coal stove that can be very subtly controlled so that it can be banked up to see you toasting through the coldest night or even be waiting with a warm greeting when you return from work. It was in a sense the modern incarnation of the camp fire.

Some boats have bigger stoves or even cooking ranges that will burn anything in their capacious fire-boxes. As Boudica was a long boat I decided to get a big cast iron range that I could use wood in. I chose to use wood primarily because it was free and I needed to live as frugally and efficiently as I could – but my stove could burn coal also. There was a big oven beside the firebox and even though I had a gas cooker most of my cooking was done on the range. This became the warm heart of my home.

Wood is mostly free – or it ought to be since millions of tons of it are thrown away. Tree wood needs to season for at least a year but storing it can be a problem. Best of all is scrap wood – the kind most people throw away and that gets buried in landfill sites. Good dry used wood has more heat in it but also nails which can clog the grate of a small stove. Only a stove with a wide grate that enables the nails to fall through with the ash can accommodate this bountiful gift. A gift for sure, because once people know that you burn wood they'll happily give you a call to get rid of it, or even better leave it on the river bank for you.

Then of course you'll have to cut it up. I used a bow saw at first but I invested in an electric saw before I got repetitive strain injury. With a tungsten-tipped blade an electric saw will soon have the wood cut into suitable lengths. Then you've got to gather it up, bag it, store it, but hey - it's free so don't complain that some work is involved.

Wood warms you twice they say and there's something rebelliously exciting about cooking your dinner on a stove powered by wood you've gathered and cut yourself. After a while you come to understand that this primaeval activity connects you to long lost feelings and emotions that everyone once had – connections to another reality. It's not as simple as flicking a switch and it takes a while to heat the boat in the morning, but you can linger beneath the duvet, doze and meditate, contemplate what you might do today, think of the money you're saving and enjoy your liberation from the utility companies.

Wood burning is labour intensive and can take over your life – especially in the Winter when stocks of wood and how dry and seasoned it is will matter a great deal to you. Also, you'll learn never to drive past a skip without looking to see if there's any wood in it. Coal is less hassle, but it's not cheap, but you could get together with other boaters and pay for a massive order in the Summer when it is cheaper. Cooperation with those around you can be so mutually beneficial - but a word of caution - this means stashing big heaps of coal bags – but stack them nearby on the river bank not on top of the boat – it may capsize!

There's something else about the stove that those who live in houses miss out on. A real fire is something elemental. It's life, warmth, safety, security – just like the camp fire that kept the wild animals away when a traveller rested for the night. Not for nothing was the hearth the spiritual centre of the home and sitting around the stove with orange flames showing through the little glass window recaptures those feelings you don't get from a blank radiator.

Trivets may appear in your life – no they are not an irritating illness, they are archaic artefacts - small practical and essential cast iron platforms wrought into decorative patterns upon which your kettles, pots and pans may simmer and rest, and you quietly wonder how you ever lived without them. When the rain has fallen hard and fast all night long pattering on the steel roof of the boat while I lay snug and warm in my artificial burrow the wood stove whispered comforting wisdoms in the darkness.

Oak logs will warm you well that are old and dry
Logs of pine will sweetly smell, but the sparks will fly
Birch logs will burn too fast, Chestnut scarce at all
Hawthorn logs are good to last – cut them in the fall
Holly logs will burn like wax you may burn them green
Elm logs like to smouldering flax no flame to be seen

Beech logs for Winter time Yew logs as well
Green Alder logs it is a crime for any man to sell
Pear logs and Apple logs they will scent your room
Cherry logs across the dogs smell like flowers of broom
Ash logs smooth and grey burn them green or old
Buy up all that come your way worth their weight in gold

-       An old verse of unknown origin

Trees and the wood they supplied were once an essential part of life. Their use was not just as fuel, for each tree had its purpose in that its wood was suited to a particular task – willow for example which grew in abundance along the rivers was used to build houses, fences, coracles and baskets as well as a plethora of household objects – but it was also a medicine - its leaves and bark a source of salicylic acid which was good for rheumatism and for general pain relief. Aspirin is derived from the willow.

Elm trees which have been all but exterminated in England now once supplied the perfect hard wood for furniture and tool handles. Oak is hard, strong and enduring and so it was used for the beams of houses as well as for building ships – in fact, the same wooden beams that were used in ship construction often ended up in houses, barns and inns, wood that served us for sometimes over a thousand years.

Trees had other attributes that are all but lost to us now. Their coming into leaf in Spring governed the correct time to plant various crops so the different species were a kind of calendar. They also had spiritual properties – the willow was associated with the Moon Goddess, the Oak with Hercules, a God of thunder and lightning, the Hawthorn with rebirth of the new year. Trees were not just there to be used, they were a sacred part of life. It's not surprising that the interior of old churches mimic the sacred groves of the old religion Christianity was imposed upon - and then there is the Yew – they too have found their place in church yards, but the Yew – which is legendary for the making of long bows - can live for thousands of years and if allowed to get old enough it would have encircling it a ring of its descendant yews remaining when the original tree died. These became natural temples of immense age and were regarded as sacred groves far, far back in time.

Around the Island there were not so many woodlands – apart from the artificial plantations and wind breaks. Real mixed woodland is getting rare anywhere in England now, but in the Fens the willow dominates the wild areas that remain – in particular the rivers. There are relatively narrow areas of woodland bordering the more remote stretches of the rivers. The willow is of course a tree that naturally thrives near water, but it's roots also help support the riverbanks as well as providing wind cover for the huge fields. In the past its branches provided just about everything the natives of these parts once needed.

The willow is a comparatively recent species on the Fens it seems for it has been discovered that up until around 4000 years ago the land was covered in huge yew tree forests that declined as the land sunk and the salt sea water invaded the low-lying land killing them when the ancient inland sea was formed. The remains of these trees are often ploughed up by farmers and are regarded as a big inconvenience as the branches and trunks are extremely hard and damage farm machinery.

It's not uncommon to see a pile of what are known as 'bog oaks' in the corner of a field. These are yews not oaks of course and some enterprising farmers sell them to garden centres which market the twisted forms as ornamental additions to gardens. These yew trees would have grown to be 20 metres high – as tall as my boat was long - and they lived for around 400 years, sometimes much longer. I've had the experience of rescuing a yew trunk from the river as it came floating by and it was incredibly dense almost like compressed coal. It was not easy to cut up but it burned very nicely.

You may have to meander into Suffolk or north Norfolk to find more mixed woodland. It can be well worth the journey for when you walk among the trees you enter a time that might be from any age for the trees and plants have been around for thousands of years longer than we have. A good place to go might be Lopham Fen where another landscape has been enviro-engineered back to the Neolithic period with facsimile horses and cattle to graze it. All woodlands have been managed to a degree, but you can still get a sense of what this land must have been like when the primaeval wildwood covered it from coast to coast.

Trees trim us down to size, they make us lower our voices, they invoke respect. One time I worked in a therapeutic community for people with mental health problems and I used to take the residents in the minibus to visit local woodlands. Walking among the trees would have a calming positive effect on them and it was far better than sitting around watching daytime TV and smoking themselves to death. They would begin to use their imagination, forget their problems and come alive again.

There are not enough trees around these days and I think that's one of the reasons why people are unhappy and confused. It's trees that connect the land to the sky, the past to the present, they hold life inside them when the Winter comes and in the Spring they let it flow right up to the sky. It's trees that teach us that people are not the highest form of life upon the Earth neither are they the most fruitful, or the most bountiful. Early spiritual practices were carried out in sacred groves and a visit to any old church will display carved stone foliage, green men and the shapes of the trees reflected in the architecture.

You are more than a ray of sunshine
I a leafless tree, you an evergreen
I tramp off the beaten path in your forest

- Nadine

The other essential in our time is electricity of course. A wise boater does his or her best to be independent of the 'leccy', but there are those who crave washing machines, flat screen TV's, immersion heaters and other 240-volt paraphernalia. This addiction they find to be something of a handicap for the temporary cessation of mains electric power on the Island was common – in fact, I recall that one boater was stuck in his boat in the nearby lock all night because a power cut rendered the lock gates stuck. Power cuts didn't affect me very much because I was prepared and I had alternative 12-volt battery electrics.

Why anyone would abandon the outside world and its ways and still want its more dubious benefits was a mystery to me, but there are those who cannot shake off the gilded chains of consumer slavery. What most boat dwellers do need however is a battery charger, which runs from 240-volt mains electricity. It is perfectly possible to do without a charger, for running the engine will charge the 12-volt batteries and a battery of solar panels on the roof will help keep them charged. 12-volt appliances, mini-inverters and LED lighting reduced the amount of leccy used to ridiculous levels too. Add a portable generator and you can tell the utility companies to disappear up their multinational profit margins. You may think there are no echoes of the past in using electricity but ironically, disconnection from the grid connects you to what I would call the Cosmic Interface – the natural power grid, ancient and self-empowering – and you don't get a final demand for it.

Another essential is knowing a good mechanic. Not being that handy with mechanical things I found it wise to have the engine maintained properly by a man who knew what he was doing. There was one such mechanic who really knew his way around narrowboats and I always paid him as soon as he'd done the job and in cash. Almost all the boats were powered by diesel engines and 'Bou' had a big old three-cylinder Lister diesel engine that thumped away all day long. Engines like this once powered all manner of machinery – generators, cement mixers, tractors, diggers, dumper trucks – the kind of working vehicles that built the modern world. The engine was air cooled there was no need for a radiator and water circulated through the engine. Cool air was drawn in from one side of the boat's engine compartment by a fan and pushed out the other side. The engine didn't rev high enough to get really hot but it did vibrate a lot and it was noisy. I reduced the noise and vibrations a little by installing an insulated false deck complete with inspection hatches. I also had the engine refurbished as it had been chugging away for over thirty years.

There were very few fuel stations on the system and what there were only seemed to be open when they felt like it so most boaters would have two or more jerry cans and take a trip to the fuel suppliers where you could get just about any fuel there is. Bou's engine mostly ran on red agricultural diesel which was cheaper than the 'white' diesel used on the road, but it was very happy with a diet of heating oil – which is basically the same thing – kerosene – it was just cheaper than the red. The engine could even run on reprocessed chip oil I was told, but I never tried it.

Filling up the boat meant unscrewing a big hexagonal cap with a monster adjustable spanner about three feet long. Then a long plastic pipe jubilee-clipped to a big orange tractor funnel was inserted into the tank and the diesel was first decanted into red plastic containers, lifted up and poured into the tractor funnel down into the tank. If you were really careful, you'd only spill a few drops but diesel is smelly so gloves and old clothes were in order. A full tank would last for ages, I would probably fill it three or four times a year and I always had a full jerry can spare. The fuel gauge was a high-tech boat hook with a mark carved on the wooden shaft. I simply dipped it in the tank.

Bou had a massive water tank in her bows which would last for over two weeks if need be however, it was wise to keep the tank full especially during the Winter when the top few inches of water froze. Most narrowboats have a comparatively small water tank under the front deck – which is most commonly known as the 'cratch' - a word left over from the times when canal boats were pulled by horses and the front area was used for hay to feed the horse. Filling the water tank with a garden hose on a reel was easy enough when moored on the Island where there were plenty of water taps.

When I went out cruising there weren't so many taps available, but there were a few moorings with water points accessible with a key to unlock the steel boxes that housed them. Of course, you had to take your hose reel along for the trip and this lived on the roof along with two wooden planks (one for each end of the boat) boat hooks, long pole, ropes and anything else you needed. If I was going to be on the river for a few days, I would take along a few bags of cut wood for the range. I would usually aim to be out for about a week although in the Summer I'd avoid the river at weekends and especially at bank holidays. This was because the river would become infested by idiots who often behaved badly and generally spoiled the experience.

For those of us who lived on the river these interlopers were most unwelcome as not only did they infect our alternative world with their 'normal' world ways they disregarded the usual rules and protocols of the waterways. Most of them were known to us as 'plastic' boaters or 'tupperware' – that is they burbled up and down in endless parades of almost identical fibreglass cruisers usually going too fast, causing damage to the river banks and upsetting nesting water birds. They also had the bad manners to moor their boats in the middle of a mooring so that other boats could not tie up. Having claimed a mooring for themselves they would set up their wind breaks, barbeques, folding chairs and tables, put on some loud music to mask the birdsong and proceed at all possible speed to get drunk.

There were a good many of these weekenders who were unable to drive on the roads under the influence of alcohol, drank excessively and behaved like geriatric Hells Angels on the river. Usually, it would be the man who drove the boat while swigging copious amounts of booze while his utterly disinterested wife would lounge around reading brainless magazines completely oblivious to the beauty and tranquillity of the river.

These people were best avoided as they seemed to forget which side of the river to drive on, they made as much noise and drove as fast as their little plastic cruisers could, disturbing the water as much as possible. They were inconsiderate of anyone else and completely ignored their own safety and that of everyone else. Also, they seemed to delight in breaking down broadside across the river whenever they could. I found it essential to stay on the Island when these people were about and enjoy the river at the times when it was safe and pleasant to go out.

Fortunately, for ninety-five percent of the time the rivers were pretty much ours – the boaters who lived on the Island and on the other colonies that had formed throughout the system. These other colonies were mostly smaller than the Island – that is there were fewer residents, fewer boats. One in particular was known as the 'splinter colony' as it had been pioneered by a few boats that had left the Island to get even further away.

However, as is the way of things the splinter colony grew along the river banks it was based on. Its facilities were few though. Other colonies had been around for many years; some were just outposts of a few boats lining a river bank.

This alternative world was ours to roam freely and it was a special feeling to meet up with friends from these other colonies, it was like going back in time to when people would have visited other far-flung villages remote in the wild woodlands when rivers were the highways and canoes, coracles and small boats brought goods to trade. It was by nature a relatively small world in which your reputation was easily known – whether good or bad, thus there existed a kind of self-policing – you behaved as you expected others to behave and in doing so you gained respect and status. If anyone accrued a bad reputation, they could be sure everyone knew about it so it was essential you conducted yourself well. I think it must have also been this way in the distant past. Again and again during my exile there came the feeling of reliving or echoing ancient ways and with those feelings came deeper understanding of our human journey especially when juxtaposed against our modern ways which seemed to have degenerated into a form of mass psychosis and lost their true essence.

There is another useful accessory although it isn't essential – a dinghy. Many of the boaters had dinghies which they used to cross the water to their moorings on the other side of the island. These were mostly old fibreglass boats that they paddled across – some had outboard motors but the distance was so short it was hardly worth the effort of starting them. I had a dinghy with an outboard loaned to me for a while and it was great to travel in it, but the motor was very unreliable so I rowed it mostly. Rowing is quite ridiculous really as you can't see where you're going, but it's a peaceful way of travelling. The nicest thing about having a small boat was that it got you very close to the water and you could stop and enjoy the river at sunset perhaps, floating on the still surface, the colours of the clouds and sky reflected, suspended between two dimensions. Now, I can't swim and I have negative buoyancy so I always wore a self-inflating life jacket when I went out in the dinghy.

Later in my time on the Island I got a small square shaped dinghy that was very stable and sometimes we would tow it behind Bou for aquatic adventures further away, but towing anything from a boat is not so easy as neither the tower or the towed has any brakes and that causes problems. In the case of moving another narrowboat with a dead engine the solution is to 'breast up' which means you simply tie the two boats together. This works very well, steering the two boats from one of them is surprisingly easy.

Believe me young friend, there is nothing – half so much worth doing as simply messing about in boats

The Wind in The Willows - Kenneth Grahame

Now, before we go any further on this odyssey, I'd like to take you on a short trip on the river so that you might get a brief insight of this new life I'd found – we'll be just a few hours out. This trip would be typical if I had visitors who wanted to get a flavour of boat life or maybe a female guest who might have other motivations. We would leave the mooring on the Island around mid-morning and slide gently past the other boats, pass under the bridge at the entrance to the marina, turn hard right, then hard left and we would be out on the main river. We pass the washes – flood plains where there are often a small herd of gorgeous horses running free, cattle from nearby farms also graze here.

There are flocks of Canada geese who take off from the river honking their annoyance. There are usually plenty of swans on this stretch, mostly adolescent groups. They are not put out by a boat chugging by, they sometimes wait until the bow of the boat nudges them aside. Swans pair for life and have a family every year. When the youngsters are full grown the parents chase them away and they collect in groups like teenagers until they eventually find the right mate. We might well get our first sight of a kingfisher or two – they fly fast and low along the riversides but they're pretty small and not so easy to see. You need to look for their flight path rather than the bird itself. There is a knack to it but once you get it, you'll see loads of kingfishers.

We cruise onward, Bou's bow barely disturbing the surface of the water, her long hull slides easily along, at her stern the prop-wash bubbles the river lazily. The washes (flood plains) pass us by and after a few gentle bends there is now a fairly straight section of river and we soon pass by another boat colony, moored end to end on the left bank of the river. These are not all 'live-aboards', most are weekend boats and plastic cruisers mixed in with the line of narrowboats of various lengths.

It is good manners on the river to slow down when passing moored boats so that you don't cause a disturbance or make unnecessary waves and so we slow down. We carry on past the boats, the banks are wooded, mostly willows and lots of vegetation, wild flowers of all kinds. On the nearside bank we pass an old wind-pump – once used to drain the surrounding land but converted now into a house known now as the Pepper Pot. Then, a little further on there is a 'winding hole' a cut in the bank that allows the space to turn a boat around, but today we are pressing on.

Around a half hour later we round a bend and there is our mooring, empty and waiting. It's a pleasant spot with overhanging weeping willows. We moor up, the sun is shining as predicted, the breeze is cool, but we've had the stove going so it's kept toasty warm inside the boat. Sandy my white cat, is particularly fond of the fencing around this mooring so he enjoys tightrope walking along the fence and giving his claws a good workout.

It's good to have a break from the thump of the engine and enjoy the birdsong. We feast on bacon and melted cheese croissants followed by real coffee. The trip has relaxed us to the extent we have an after-lunch sleep. We wake slowly, drowsy but replete, the sun is still with us. There is sufficient width of the river to spin Bou around for the return. A rope around a mooring post and with the tiller hard over and with some power from the engine she slowly turns, her bow pointing back the way we came. We cast off for the slow chug back to the Island. Kingfishers patrol the river's edges; white terns dive for the swarms of silver fish Bou has gently herded ahead of us, a family of swans fly close by almost near enough to touch, swallows and dragonflies visit, fluorescent blue damselflies hitch hike on Bou's roof. It's good to be on the river and good to be going back home.

After a dreamy time on the tiller, I get to have a break sitting on the front deck while one of my guests takes over – which is a fun experience for them and great for anyone's confidence. Bou is easy to steer – in a relatively straight line at least - and there is a brass bell to ring if my relief has any problems. Sitting right up front you are so close to the river. It's quiet too, just the burble of the water at her bow, the river like a mirror and we move as if travelling along the seam between two dimensions. Looking down through the clear water you can see all kinds of fish swimming among the green weed forests – another world within another world.

Eventually the washes appear again thronged with geese nesting among the rough grass, soon there will be five or six big white eggs in each of their nests. You could take one of two and they'll conveniently lay a few more. We were not short of geese anyway. Soon the Island is coming up ahead and we slow and turn into the marina entrance, creeping under the bridge very slowly now – you might meet another boat coming out - past the lines of boats on each side then slow right down bringing her to a stop by reversing the gear. Picking the exact place by the jetty I reverse carefully and turn her swinging on the old tires fixed on the end of the jetty. It's a slow business rather like a ten-point turn, but neighbours come out to assist, catching a mooring rope and soon we are snug against the jetty again, the trip is over.

We feel satisfied and complete. I pump the stern gland replenishing the propeller shaft with fresh grease and plug in the leccy, coil the long mooring ropes on the roof and check the fore and aft mooring ropes are secure on their rings. The engine cools, I can relax. Time for another cuppa and to readjust. The visitors depart their horizons broadened. Female guests usually lingered longer and often return and serve as crew.

Gun till do cheum as gach cearn fo rionnag iuil an dachaidh
May your steps return from all the corners of the globe under
the guidance of the star that points to home

-    Gaelic saying

Waterworld

Water – some wit once said – is the solution to everything. It's everywhere of course, but you are never more aware of it than when you live upon it. Yes, the boats float upon it and it surrounds the Island, but it falls from the sky often and the level of the river rises and falls. The water is in constant motion. It is the wind upon its surface that gives it its ever-changing form and with those changes comes the rich variations of colour and light, the reflections of sky, cloud and the boats, distorted, splintered shapes, ripples, brilliant sun sparkles. Images from the gallery of the greatest artist – nature - to treasure and wonder at.

When the solid ground is beneath our feet we can feel rooted and trapped but on the water everything has the potential to move – just like we as a species once moved. The water is in us, in the clouds above, the trees and plants all around, it ripples and reflects, moves, breathes, loves. Those that live upon the land have their feet planted firmly upon it, those who live on the water feel it beneath the boat's hull, we feel our home gently move as we move around it and we are aware that we are free moving, not fixed to the land but incumbent upon the living water.

We are attracted to water in many ways. As children we find it irresistible. Life itself is completely dependent upon it. In the distant past when this land was covered in dense forests, the native people built villages beside the rivers and even on stilts in the rivers and lakes. They lived on and from the river and they travelled along it and so there is this link deep inside us that connects us to the beauty, the sustaining bounty, the safety of the river.

There was a great deal of wildlife that lived in relative harmony with the boaters; swans, geese, ducks, coots, all kinds of water fowl as well as kingfishers, woodpeckers, collared doves, goldfinches, wrens, blue tits, willow warblers – and there were of course predominantly willow trees on the Island and along the rivers. 'The Wind in the Willows' is a wonderful book to many, but when you live with that sound – or should I say sounds - you have an orchestra that plays symphonies in dancing leaves, slender bending branches. I listened to that music while the birds sang along; cuckoo, willow warbler, blackbird, wren, kingfisher, a thousand others embroidered the sighing willow strings, harmonies, syncopation, melodies only the Universe could score, I listened. I closed my eyes and felt the sun warm upon my face, light flashing from the water, the breeze upon my cheek, I listened. You could really listen - for there was no traffic noise, no trucks blundering their way to supermarkets laden with consumer tat. You could actually listen to what the human ear is designed to hear, what the human mind can deal with.

When you really think about it, the 'civilised' world is full of sounds we are not equipped to hear – no wonder it induces stress. Music is a strange thing when you think about it. Where did it originate from? The kind of music that comes from radios and movies is as far removed from the true origins of music as could possibly be imagined. Music can evoke all manner of emotions, it can be drums that induce trance, the 'Ride of the Valkyries' played in the headphones of a Nazi tank invading Poland, it can be the love one feels holding a newborn baby, it can be a wedding dance, a funeral march, a fanfare or a bugle call.

All music must have had its origins in natural sound – wind, rain, running water, birdsong, thunder perhaps. Yet we seem to have lost our appreciation and understanding of that original music – so much so that we don't even recognize it as music at all. For a man like me who had been interested in creating music most of my life this was another learning, another aspect turned on its head and now seen in its real form. There were to be so many things I would learn to see from a different perspective.

On the river time itself was elastic, nothing like the strict linear restrictive discipline it is in the outer world. When I first ventured forth upon the river, I thought it useful to time my journeys, but surprisingly it proved impossible to do so. I simply forgot; my mind had engaged with other things. I had entered another level of consciousness. I learned to be aware of the position of the sun, the degree of light left. It became my clock, the moon measured the nights, the sun and stars the seasons of the year. It's a revelation how liberating it is to be free of the clock, to live in natural time as we once did and had always done.

It was originally the Christian Church who first commissioned clocks to be made – so that they knew when to hold services. Then they stuck the clock on the church tower so that the peasants could get off their backs and into the fields on time. The clock became a slave driver from then on – especially during the Industrial Revolution when the railways forced a strict standardisation of time over the whole country. Now in the digital age the clock still regulates people's lives. To me this seems a kind of imprisonment, a kind of slavery we've accepted. Why should our lives be divided up and regulated by those who want to control us? We don't even think about the tyranny of the clock until we spend some free time without its dictatorship.

There are countless other tyrannies we've come to accept and are not even aware of until we experience how things were. I once came across a very old pub in a remote Suffolk village that was unchanged for maybe two hundred years. It had been deliberately kept and maintained as pubs used to be, no TV, no game machines, no bar even - just a tap room with beer in barrels, real log fires and wooden benches in petitioned booths so people could sit, talk and eat. You could easily imagine how it was when people travelled by horse or on foot breaking their journey at the pub, meeting, exchanging news, gossip, doing business maybe. By the very nature of the interior you were made welcome as a human being - not a cash cow to be milked. The seating invited conversation, human contact, the food was English and home cooked. Living history. In my own way I was attempting to recapture something of the old ways of living on the Island. I was returning to basic things, rejecting the trivia of modern land living and to my surprise by rejecting these things I was discovering the real treasures that have been lost to us.

Would you like to know the history of our present miseries? Here it is –
There existed a natural man; an artificial man was introduced within this man;
And within this cavern a civil war breaks out which lasts for life.

-    Dennis Diderot. French Philosopher 1784

Having visitors was always a good excuse to get out on the river and as long as I had someone to share the journey with I would get out there as much as I could. There was the whole river system to explore and I never tired of repeating my journeys for each trip was different depending on the time of year and who accompanied me. Some of the people who had boats moored on the Island did not live there but would come at weekends or holiday times to enjoy the river. Some of them were crazy about exploring the extensive canal system which goes all over England and Wales. Getting onto the canal system was however a somewhat arduous trip through what was known as the 'middle levels' which is an area of drainage channels.

These are in my opinion immensely boring to travel along and Bou being such a long boat would have had difficulty negotiating right angle bends and low bridges. There are some very pleasant stretches of the canal system so I can appreciate why some people cruised them, but for me they had no appeal. I saw nothing exciting about chugging through the often-dangerous industrial deserts of the Midlands, traversing the ancient claustrophobic tunnels or arguing with maniac holiday boaters at the locks. I much preferred the Fens, the river system that was close at hand. There were many gorgeous places to visit and get myself far from the madding crowd.

When I went to live on the Island, I was told about a very special river which people referred to as if it was something magical. The more I heard about this river the more it assumed the character of a mythical place – a kind of Shangri-la.

Naturally I was keen to travel to this idyllic, heaven on Earth, but it was sometime before I actually made the trip. The weather had to be right and I was assured the best time to go was at the end of Summer when the trees started to change their colours. It was easy to get to - in fact I'd passed by the reed bound entrance quite a few times when I'd chugged up to the sluices at the edge of the system. I examined it thoroughly in the 'Blue book' – which was a mine of information (most of it years out of date) about the accessible rivers on the Fens. I learned from the book and by talking to former explorers that the river passed through a sugar factory, past an island and there were some spectacular lakes - that there was another boat colony, that the trees were gorgeous and the whole river was very different from the other fenland rivers.

At last, the day arrived and after a leisurely chug which took the best part of the day my crew and I slowly edged through the narrow reed festooned entrance to the river. It's narrow, twisty and very reedy at first, but after a while you pass under a railway bridge and then there is a sharp right-hand turn. There are some very nice moorings here with gorgeous weeping willow trees. I'd been advised that this was a good place to moor up for the night. After the long trip it made sense to do this and explore the rest of the river upstream the next day. This isn't a long river and you can go all the way upstream and back in a day. However, once you've been as far as you can go there's not much point in going that far again as it gets very narrow. Most people therefore, travel as far as the lakes then turn around and come back.

Early in the morning we set off. The river gets twisty and narrow with lots of trees and for some inexplicable reason you get the impression you are going downhill though you are actually going upstream. Then the first boats appear, old boats left to rot mostly. There is something sad about an abandoned boat – it's an analogy of a lost life. Boats are built to travel after all, they're meant for fun, good times, river holidays, pick-nicks, laughter in the sunshine. But among these old boats there are some that are loved and are used. Some even have full time residents. We pass them by with a wave and pass under a road bridge to find an attractive village with more boats, nearly all very smart, well looked after, their shapes and bright colours reflected in the water.

Chugging onward we leave this glimpse of civilization behind. The river is gorgeous here, a little wider, the banks lined with deciduous trees, their leaves beginning to turn, a welcome relief from the willows that are prevalent on other rivers on the system. Beyond them the landscape has ancient pasture fields where fat cattle graze on lush grass and wildflowers in the water meadows. The river twists, the trees right to the water's edge, so close you can tie up to them and hide beneath their branches if you've a mind to. Onward we go, the leaves shimmering in the light, the water flows with a purposeful current – not fast, but with intention. A grass snake with the intention of crossing to the opposite bank writhes its way through the water. We pass an ancient pumping station which would someday make a wonderful house for someone with the time and the money to convert it. At present it is home to a barn owl.

Now we see an incongruous vision – the sugar factory. There doesn't seem to be any buildings as such. It looks like something from a 1950's sci-fi movie – shapes like upended boilers, tangles of pipes, chimneys and high galleries of steel. Under a gantry we go, just clearing it with Bou's cabin roof. It carries a big hot air duct – big enough to walk through - across the river to a collection of greenhouses. The greenhouses grow vegetables – a by-product of the factory which processes sugar beet – which is a plentiful crop in these parts. Trucks and tractors come from miles around crammed with beet at the season it's harvested, but there is no steam coming from the big chimneys at present. When it's in production there are big plumes of billowing steam coming out of them and you can smell the pungent aroma of hot sugar.

We glide through a tree lined tunnel and ahead there is a narrow tree covered island which we pass on the left-hand side, on our right the side of the factory towers above us, pipes and walkways, puffs of steam, more pipes – a strange contradiction. Then under another bridge and another huge pipe that carries the dusty remnants of the sugar beet across the river and deposits it in huge heaps. Trucks take it away - but I have no idea what it's used for – maybe fertiliser, but it's all an organic process with no damaging pollution.

We slide under the last concrete road bridge and we enter a magical place. The river has widened into a gorgeous tree fringed lake. After the confining borders of the river this is wonderful – so much space and the sky reflected in its mirrored surface. This long lake is used by the sugar factory workers fishing club. We cruise onward, the lake narrowing until we are back to a river again. The landscape has changed now – it's wilder, there are different trees and waterside plants bordering the fields.

The first time I did this trip I went all the way to the end of the navigable river where I had to make a hundred-point turn to turn Bou around before heading back downstream. There is a caravan site and a riverside Marina beyond the next village, but after my first expedition I usually went to a secluded mooring spot before the village or turned around at the lakes. Now chugging down-stream we pass the sugar factory again and retrace our journey enjoying the gorgeous countryside again, not a house or a soul in sight, just the water birds, swans, the odd swimming grass snake crossing in our wake. The sun sparkles on the water, the white clouds drift slowly in long lines like ripples on a big blue beach - magical.

Eventually we return to the same moorings we departed from to spend the night. It's a really nice spot, peaceful and wild. At night you can hear the barking of wild deer. There are masses of elderberry bushes bordering the woodland set back from the bank which is higher than the land. We used to make a liqueur called 'Elderberry rob' which is a wonderful natural medicine for colds and flu and so we would sit on the bank separating the berries from their stalks with a table fork. When we return to the island we'll wash them, boil them up with sugar on the range then bottle and store them for the Winter.

So, what did I think about the journey? Well, it was indeed wonderful and it was a very different river from the other rivers on the system, but now the mythical place was no longer a myth and even though I would subsequently travel there again many times after my first trip I couldn't help but feel a sense of loss. I remember as a child there was a place that was round a bend in the road that I'd never seen. I fantasised what might be there and it became an almost magical place purely because it was unseen and unknown and could have been a place filled with all manner of wonders. When I eventually went around that bend my fantasies were destroyed, never to be real to me again. There have been other places that I've come across – roads that I'd seen in passing but never explored which seemed to hold the same magic and in some cases I chose not to venture there preferring to retain my fantasies.

The world was once like that, full of places that were unknown, places that we imagined, all kinds of strange sights, peoples and animals existed in these fantasies. Mountains that people revered as the homes of their Gods were never climbed – they were sacred. Now we know the whole world, we can sit at home and use Google Earth to look down like Gods on any spot we may choose, we've been to the Moon, sent rovers to Mars, toured the Solar System and in doing so we've destroyed the magic of our imagination and the realities of our fantasies. I can remember what science fiction was like before we actually went into space. How rich and diverse the planets were in those stories from the 1950's. It's been a bit of an anti-climax to find no Martians on Mars and no green skinned Mekon on Venus. The outer space that Dan Dare explored in the 'Eagle' comic I read as a kid is just a collection of rocky, icy, lifeless balls.

Reality – the unhappy child of many illusions - is what we're left with and reality is not always pleasant, not only that reality destroys the sacred, kills the imagination, devalues the power of myth and cuts us off from other truths – those that come from our other sources – feelings, intuitions and our collective consciousness, our racial memory perhaps, the repository of all human knowledge and experience that we once all shared but now only glimpse in our dreams. What is there now that we can call sacred, where are the Shangri-La's, the Eldorado's, where are the places only the God's can live? I think we inwardly grieve for these magical places and sometimes wish we could have our lives again enriched by our ignorance.

-    The Two Voices - Tennyson

Long before I moved to the river at a time in my life where I was relatively content, I lived in a small village that was bisected by a very busy road. On the other side of this road was a really nice area – a former country estate where we would take a walk at the weekend or in the Summer evenings. Our usual route took us through fields of sheep, past a farm and across a rather mystical place. There was a stream that divided and then joined together again making a roughly diamond shaped grassy area edged by beautiful mature sycamores. The foot path crossed this island by two wooden foot bridges. The branch of the stream that ran under the first bridge was the lesser of the two, it flowed without the same purpose as the water beneath the second bridge. By standing still upon this bridge I could actually feel the living energy of the stream in the core of my body. The water bubbled and sang over the stones in its bed, there were shingle and pools, exposed tree roots even in one place a fallen tree that connected one side to the other.

There was one very special tree that lived upon the side where the stream did not display its energy and I wonder now if this tree was the reason. We found that there was a part of its massive trunk where individually we could sit comfortably and be embraced and supported by the living tree. You could feel the energy coming from within the tree – a life force certainly but more than that – the tree communicated its wisdom, its actual being and identity, its life experiences. It defies explanation in mere words for there are none to describe such things - they simply *are* and you cannot believe in their existence unless you experience them yourself. I think the ability to connect with the natural world in this way was once available to everyone. It's one of the many natural gifts we have either lost or have been buried by the way we live today.

The life force of the river could be felt as soon as Bou left the Island and set out on the main river – it was the same force I'd experienced before over the stream but this time it was much stronger. After all, a river is far bigger than a stream and as such it surely carries the force from the thousands of streams that join with it. The river spoke to me in its own way as it took the boat along, the engine chugged, the prop turned, the water bubbled gently behind, the ripples from the long hull caressed the river's silver skin as we slowly accelerated to a speed no more than a steady walking pace.

Bou's rudder had angled steel plates welded on it that directed the thrust from the prop downwards and this had the effect of disturbing the surface to a minimum. The hull narrowed a little towards the bow and this too meant she slid through the water with minimum disturbance. On a still morning when the river was a liquid mirror it seemed almost sacrilegious to disturb the surface, yet looking back at the wake the river recorded her passing with the gentlest ripples and wavelets that barely rocked the reeds.

One time when I was on the river, I noticed what I thought was a flock of birds in the distance, but I was wrong – I was heading into a huge swarm of Fenland bees. I could do nothing to avoid them, they are big and aggressive so I was forced to shut the engine down and leave the tiller to seek refuge in the cabin.

Fortunately, they buzzed off before Bou crashed into the river bank and I could emerge and take control again, but it was very scary. It was one of those incidents that remind you this is still a wild country and nature has its dangerous side as well as the benign face it usually presents. Once people believed nature had to be honoured and placated otherwise, she would destroy you and back then there were many ways nature could wipe you out.

When you are a fit and healthy human being living in the 21st century you don't understand how delicately life and death are balanced. Unless you are old and frail the Winter is not going to kill you because we have warm homes to protect us, but back in the Neolithic the Winter was the time of death. The frozen death culled the weak, the old, the sick and the injured people, birds and animals alike. With the advent of agriculture, it must have taken enormous pressure to induce former nomads to remain in one place throughout the year. One important factor in bringing about these changes may well have been religion. After all, the nomad moved with seasonal migrations of the animal herds and could not risk abandoning that life unless there were some very strong reasons for doing so.

A species that has learned over thousands of years that to move was to live and to stop meant death had to undergo dramatic psychological changes. Think about this – the nomad tribe could not stop on its journey for it was bound to the movement of the herd of animals they were tied to. Those people might pause for a day or two and pitch their tents but they could not linger. That meant any member of the tribe that fell ill or got too old to keep walking had to be left behind, just like those animals in the herd that were killed by predators. This harsh fact of life seems to us today as inhuman, but it has really only been the influence of Christianity that has caused us to care for the sick, have compassion and live by the moral codes we know. Before the adoption of that religion those morals we now base our society on were unheard of, utter brutality and the survival of the strongest and fittest were the way of things.

We know from anthropologists that the Neolithic hunter gatherers believed in an afterlife as they buried their dead with artefacts that would be required beyond this life and it appears that this practice continued. We also know that they built stone circles – cosmic computers - that marked out the progress of the year, the seasons, the signs in the stars. You can understand how a once nomadic community needed to be reassured by their priests that the sun would return and life would renew after the death period of Winter. These early settlers were dependent on their religious leaders to show them when it was mid-Winter, mid-Summer, when to plant their crops, when to slaughter their animals – their existence utterly depended on this knowledge. The priests must have been regarded as very powerful, magical even for they had the skills to read the stars.

The early farming societies were utterly dependent on the sun and they regarded it as a God who gave life to everything. In the Winter they noted that the Sun God's path through the heavens declined and its life-giving warmth ebbed away. To ensure the return of the sun they gave a sacrifice at the Summer Solstice – when the sun attained its most northerly station. In some parts of Europe they selected only the finest, strongest, most handsome young man – a 'king' who would be worthy after his death to mate with the white Moon Goddess. They deduced that this 'Sun King' was imprisoned by her in the north – the place where the sun never shone and from where the frozen winds and snows of Winter came. Thus, the representative of the Sun God was killed at mid-Summer and reborn at mid-Winter. His death would hopefully bring forth a good harvest.

The gruesome barbaric practice of human sacrifice by various methods eventually died out especially with the advent of

Christianity. Jesus Himself took on the sacrifice, but even today remnants of this belief system survive, in the burying of corn dollies (replica babies) in the last field to be harvested. The Roman Sun God was known as Apollo and it was common to bury a child beneath a new building to ensure protection against bad luck. Even today some builders carry on the tradition by putting a few coins beneath the hearth of a new house – a token sacrifice to ensure good fortune.

We are incredibly fortunate to live in the time that we do, but we don't appreciate our survival or give thanks for it. My time in the wilderness taught me to give thanks with every dawn and sunset, thanks for another day of life. If you live for 75 years you will have the opportunity to witness 27,375 dawns and the same number of sunsets - that's 54,750 times to honour the turning of the Earth. That is of course if the skies are not clouded over. It sounds a lot, but how many of us count the days of our lives with such sanctity?

As for the chance to glory in the sight of a full moon, then there are just 900 times you might see it rise orange and mysteriously grow brighter to flood the night with silver magic – again providing the sky is clear. Yet the moon was for thousands of years a Goddess to be worshipped, we used her to govern our lives, plant our crops, measure the seasons and we even sacrificed human beings to her to ensure our survival – for maybe ten thousand years we believed this was essential for our crops to grow, our domesticated animals to remain alive and for our societies to prosper.

The King is dead – Long live the King.

It's worth remembering the next time you see a full moon rise that thousands of deaths were thought necessary to ensure prosperity. In a sense that is still true for warfare which involves the sacrifice of thousands of mostly young men is the mechanism that all modern economies are based upon. When humans were nomadic there seemed to be little reason or necessity to waste time and energy in conflict – merely surviving was enough to occupy their lives.

It appears that only when the nomadic ways ceased and people settled that warfare truly began to preoccupy them. Settled communities were forced to lay in food stocks to see them through the Winter months. Those assets required protection - which meant walls had to be built and full-time defenders were needed along with administrators and weapons manufacturers otherwise a stronger, predatory tribe might simply pillage what it needed.

Gone forever was the nomad's tribal leader or chief who usually achieved his status because of his strength and wisdom. Now the head of the community had to serve multiple functions as the layers of administration increased, each position becoming essential to the functioning of the ever more complex social structure. The new villages and towns were forced to develop top heavy hierarchies of non-productive inhabitants who controlled and governed those who actually worked to feed, defend and sustain the whole community and it was and still is the young men who are sacrificed.

It only stands to reason that where there's sacrifice, there's someone collecting the sacrificial offerings. Where there's service, there is someone being served. The man who speaks to you of sacrifice is speaking of slaves and masters, and intends to be the master.

-    Ayn Rand

The landscape of the Fens could seem flat and dreary at times, but the skies – oh the skies, more than compensated. For one thing the skies are huge with nothing much to impede them from the far horizons and the clouds are often spectacular formations of tumbling fantasy castles and cities ever changing, the sunsets and dawns would give John Constable heartaches of frustration. I've always loved to look at the sky – it communicates so much mood, the portents predicting the weather of course, but there are messages, feelings, wisdoms that are displayed there. The sky is another world above us which most people seem to be largely unaware of, but surely it cannot be good to ignore that which we call heaven. There are whole landscapes up there, oceans, continents, islands, archipelagos and even deserts that constantly change and mutate, wonderful colours and shades. There is the true majesty of nature up there and unless we fly in a plane we can only look up and wonder at it. However, living on the water everything up there is reflected – so you get twice as much to wonder at.

Cool are the winds that push the cloud shadows across the flat landscape and tremble the topmost branch-fingers where wax buds strain to split to the sun spill, between the white cumulus sailing the blue ocean heavens. Blossom white on the twisted hawthorn, ancient hedge rowed green browed child leafed soften the stunted form and in the columned halls of woodlands the sap rises, the new life swells, the grey-brown leaf carpets reveal crowded new green spiked seekers of light. Flowers push up through the rich earth, the whole world becomes greener, the weather changes, skies get bluer. The Earth has turned back again as it spins on its yearly orbit of the blazing star that gives us life.

When I was a child, I loved to look at the sky, I was fascinated by the clouds that passed over me and I learned about them and what they signified. I yearned to be among them, to see them from above. I watched movies and read about aviation whenever

I could. I learned all I could about flying but I came to realise that there was not much chance of me ever learning to fly – I would never cope with the necessary mathematics that I would need to navigate my way around the sky and of course I could never have afforded to take lessons.

I used to regularly dream that I was capable of flight, that there was an area inside the core of my body that I could activate that would enable me to rise up and fly at will. Of course, when I woke up it was hard to reconcile that I had been merely dreaming for it seemed so real. Flying dreams are not unusual, many people have them, but what do they represent? Are we somehow remembering a time in the past when we were actually capable of levitation? I read somewhere that there were Tibetan monks who could cover huge distances by travelling through the air as a result of training their minds to overcome physical limitations. Perhaps the dreams represent a longing to reach heaven – a spiritual elevation. Whatever the dreams represent there is the sense of loss on awakening and a lost sense of ecstasy and freedom that haunts you.

I was in my mid-forties before I actually flew in a plane. My first flight didn't last very long as it happened, for on take-off when the passenger jet was climbing steeply an inconsiderate seagull decided to fly up one of the engines causing a huge bang and scaring everyone into stunned silence. Reassuringly, the fully loaded plane still went up like a rocket on its remaining engine before returning to the airport for an emergency landing. I was quite stressed by this event but not deterred for once everyone had boarded another plane we continued our journey without any more mishaps. I was rewarded by the spectacle of flying through and above the clouds, looking down at the Earth remote below. It was wonderful, incredible - yet my fellow passengers thought no more about it than travelling on a bus and consequently didn't bother to look out of the windows.

Some years later I took another flight on a vintage biplane. That was really flying, just as the pioneers of aviation experienced. The ancient machine rattled and shuddered when it taxied to the runway but once it was airborne it was as steady as a rock. I must say though that looking at the sky from the ground is to experience the real magic, as our forebears did. For them the heavens were the realm of the Gods where thunderstorms, rainbows, eclipses, halos and sundogs could only be imagined as miraculous manifestations of spiritual consequences and omens to be heeded – and the night skies were a mystery that could only be interpreted by myths born from an overwhelming awe.

On the river I felt that awe to a degree. The sky, the weather, the colours spoke to me as they had when I was a child. Waking early to witness the dawn became a daily ritual, a time to communicate with the Universe; the music of birdsong, the breath of a gentle breeze rippling the water, fragmenting colours, yellows, golds, oranges, salmon pink cloud reflections.

I would sit on the front deck and let it all sink into me and give no thought about those who were gulping a hurried breakfast while the TV news spewed lies and destruction before rushing off to the hell of their own personal hamster wheels. I gave thanks that I wasn't one of them anymore, but at least they had the Island to return to when they'd finished the purgatory of their work and a boat they could cruise on at the weekend or their holiday period.

Here on the water, there was no alarm clock to shatter your dreams, no numbers on a calendar to tick off, the time was measured by natural pointers; blackbird song accompanied my slow awakening and later the wrens were surprisingly loud for such a tiny bird, then goldfinches twittered in the hedgerows, the fleeting squeak of a kingfisher, sometimes the patter of otter cubs playing over the deck. In the Spring the cuckoo announced its arrival, evocative, timeless, soothing, dreamy sounds that you lie in your warm bed and enjoyed, embraced - and all year round there was the cooing of our resident collared doves.

The world was talking to me softly, in words unheard, in feelings that were sometimes impossible to define. They are so ancient. They mingled with my drowsy mind wanderings, the morning's cosmic news broadcast borne on the Universal tides of connection, informing, communicating, enriching, eternal visions, dramas, symphonies, the music of the spheres. Was I the only one receiving? What did it say?

I'm looking at clouds drifting and changing rolling along see how they fly. Colours and light, castles and canyons islands and streams in an ocean of sky. Distant lands existing way up high, lost horizons day dreams passing by.

I look at the world, I look at the people going somewhere. see how they run. Searching to find a truth they can cling to wandering around looking for someone. Is there something missing they don't see? Or is there some connection lost on me?

I look to the stars the mystery eternal diamond infinity, see how they shine. How many worlds are spinning around them, how far away through space and through time. Countless computations going on, endless permutations of the One.

I'm looking at clouds, I'm looking at rainbows I'm looking at sunsets, gazing at stars
I think it's a shame that so many people can't stop what they're doing and see where they are.
It might be a useful point of view, to look beyond the clouds for something new

Clouds - Les Richards

Imagine if you had lived all your life in a huge, gloomy castle and you'd had no idea that there existed a whole bright and wonderful world outside of its stone walls – everything you knew was contained within that fortress. That would understandably be seen as a limited perspective. Now imagine that one day – quite by chance - you come across an open window and you see for the first time that there exists a whole new world beyond the castle and through that window you see the sun rising over a beautiful landscape and you see there a shining river meandering off into the far distance. Would you forget about what you'd seen through the window? No, I don't think anyone in that scenario could forget. I think anyone who had seen through that window would have to go out there, leave the castle and explore that new world.

Sure, you might be a little scared to leave behind all that you had known, but the temptation would overwhelm any reluctance, the brightness, the colours, the lure of the unknown, the possibilities, the chance of adventure would call to you and you could not resist. For one thing this discovery might cause you to ask why you had spent your life shut away from this outer world, you might ask yourself why you hadn't been told about it or you might be suspicious that the truth of this reality had been kept from you. You might come to realise that although a fortress will protect you, its walls can also be a prison.

This was how it was for me. I had found a window on some other world and I was bound to explore it. The river was there to be travelled and I had a boat to sail upon it. Where would it take me? I had no idea at first, but once I had left the old world behind, I could not return, I could not un-see what I'd seen and as time went by and I began to learn more and more there was no way I could ever unlearn the things I discovered. This is a journey you can never return from – which was exactly what I needed.

I was fortunate to be living in an area quite unlike anywhere else on Britain's waterways. This particular system of rivers and drainage channels was kept at a reasonable balanced level by sluice barriers and locks at its extremities. Excess water falling as rain was diverted away from the system onto huge flood plains outside it through long straight drainage channels.

This was all pretty effective but the English weather is capricious to say the least. Sometimes there were such vast amounts of rain that the sluices couldn't cope with it and there was flooding (as in the day I moved there) the excess water flowing clear over the barriers into the river channels that were subject to tidal influence.

A trip I made often was to the northern limit of the system where the sluice complex marked the boundary between the tidal and non-tidal river systems. Apart from the first river (where the Island was) the journey was on a really wide waterway which meant it was easy to turn Bou around if need be. There were also several decent mooring opportunities where we could stop for a break. The trip took around four or five hours depending on how often and how long I might stop on the way. That made it suitable for a leisurely, not too early departure and perhaps just one night out to return the next morning.

The river close to the sluice complex was even wider and there were plenty of moorings available on both sides where boats could wait before travelling through the locks on to the tidal rivers beyond and eventually on to the nationwide canal system. The skies here were truly enormous, reflecting in the wide waters and the landscape was open giving a wonderful sense of space. There was also a sense of being on the edge of one world where the departure point for the other world beyond beckoned.

The first time I made this trip in the company of a friend's boat I was amazed by the sluice complex engineering that controlled the levels of the waters and kept the system from flooding. Beyond the barriers with the locks that allowed boats on to the tidal rivers there were dead straight channels miles long that took excess water far away to distribute on the fields during the Winter. In the past these flooded areas were used for ice skating in the frozen Winters. At the barrier there was even a tunnel that took excess water far away to Essex. This tunnel was emptied now and then for maintenance and the engineers used bicycles to travel along it.

My most memorable impression though was waking up just before the sun rose the next morning and witnessing a misty, purple dawn reflected in the still waters. I'd never seen a dawn like it. I imagined that I was the only person alive to experience it and in a sense I was - as it was an analogy of my new life supplied by the Universe for me to witness. It is so very good for us to contemplate the beginning of a new day - it's an opportunity for everyone to welcome the very first morning of the rest of our lives.

Most people have busy lives and they simply don't have the time to honour the start and end of the day. I was fortunate to be able to do just this and I still do. It's the perfect time to meditate, think and to connect with the natural world and the Universe – it's a good time to give thanks for what we have. Being alive and able to begin a new day is a privilege because although we may not like to think about it, the day will come when we don't wake up, there will be no more days to honour. I think it's good to make the days we have as good as we can make them for ourselves and those other people we come across and to remember even when we have a disastrous day and it seems things could not be any worse. There is another day tomorrow.

Run down your stairway come out into the sun, today is the very first morning
Yesterday's history the future has begun, today is the very first morning
Open up your eyes it's very first morning,
The very first morning of the rest of your life

Leave that ol' sleepy headed fool you used to know, today is the very first morning
Something's there waiting for you to get it on, today is the very first morning
Open up your eyes it's the very first morning,
The very first morning of the rest of your life
Ask yourself what it is you're living for, today is the very first morning
Leave a note grab your coat you ain't coming back no more,
Today is the very first morning,
Open up your eyes it's the very first morning, The
very first morning of the rest of your life

-    The Very First Morning - Les Richards

One Winter day – I think it was my second Winter on the Island, I was taking my regular exercise walk. The Island was quite a wild place then and there were maybe only fifty boats moored there so there were stretches of my circular walk that were devoid of people – it was just the river and trees for company. I suddenly stopped walking and my eyes filled with tears. I came to the realisation that I was happy. Yes, for the first time in my life I was actually happy and I also realised that I hadn't known before that very moment that I had never been happy. My unhappiness died then. Sure, there had been odd times when I imagined that I'd been happy but until that moment I was stopped in my tracks on the river bank I hadn't known real happiness – and do you know I was fifty-nine years old. I hope you don't leave it so long to find transformation and happiness.

In the Winter the skies seemed even bigger and from my favourite mooring near the sluices I often watched thousands of crows fly from out of the sunset and come to gather on the telephone lines on the opposite bank before departing to their roosts in a clump of tall trees in the darkening east. There too you could watch the white barn owl patrolling the fields in the fading light. Strange birds are crows. I once witnessed a huge procession of what must have been literally millions of crows flying in a stream so long I never saw the beginning or the end of it. In mythology crows are associated with death and as messengers to the afterlife – probably because they'll eat carrion. Somehow when you see them in their huge flocks you get the feeling they are acting as a composite being, but they are noisy and argumentative when they roost which doesn't suggest a harmonious existence.

I only took Bou beyond the sluice a couple of times but I found it pretty uninspiring to be honest, so I would usually moor close to the wilder side of the river where there were really secure moorings, it was safe for Sandy my cat to explore and we were less likely to be bothered by cars passing by on the narrow road on the opposite bank. A day or two here at any time of year was really good. You could watch boats coming and going meet up with other nomads but there was still the sense of being out in the wild, close to nature.

At night the sky was dark enough to see all the stars and the Milky Way – a rare treat to be away from the usual light pollution. What could be better than to lay in bed watching the bright fleeting streaks of shooting stars through the boat's windows. These bits of rock come from who knows where in the vastness of space, they're the detritus left over from the formation of the planets and moons of our local Solar System – who knows how many billions of miles they've travelled and for how long? They're nomads too and it's surprising how many you can see – the only downside is you tend to stay awake to watch for the next one and you end up getting over tired before finally falling asleep.

I decided I would get myself a powerful telescope. I already had a decent pair of binoculars which were good for bird watching and checking out boats in the distance but no use for anything astronomical. The problem is that the more powerful they are the more difficult it is to see an object without the image shaking. Of course, a boat is not always stable and there isn't the space for a telescope and tripod of any decent size. I ended up with a small telescope that fitted on a small tripod as well as a collapsible camera tripod. This thing had a zoom lens which was OK for looking at the moon, but as for the planets there's still the problem of the shaky image. We don't often get really clear skies in England and you really need to get as far away from light pollution as you can, but this is practically impossible. The best I managed was seeing Jupiter and its moons – at least some of them – strung out either side like jewels on a fragile necklace. It's like seeing another planetary system, something so far away, yet our own solar system is just a tiny, insignificant point in the cosmos. As for the Milky way that is the ghostly light from our own galaxy. How many millions more are there and do other conscious beings gaze up into the night sky and wonder?

What lies behind us and what lies before us
Are tiny matters compared to what lies within us

R.W. Emerson

You can drive yourself crazy thinking about life, the Universe and our existence. These are things I pondered a great deal throughout my life – mainly I think it was because I seemed to blunder from one disaster to another, but a great many people give these things no thought at all – I wonder if they're better off that way? It seems to me miraculous that we are here on this unique planet as a consequence of billions of years of seemingly haphazard and random circumstances. Why did the tiny furry creatures that existed at the time of the dinosaurs evolve eventually into primates and then into human beings? The odds are literally astronomical. Why were these ape descended creatures able to populate the entire planet and even leave it to venture into the cosmos itself? Why do we exist at all? Is there a reason for our existence or is the whole thing the result of random coincidences? Such thoughts crave answers - but although science can speculate how this happened they can't tell us why.

So, I walk on uplands unbounded and know that there is hope
For that which thou didst mould out of dust To
  have consort with things eternal.

-    The Dead Sea Scrolls

Time passes and one stunningly beautiful morning, with barely a breath of breeze, the water a barely shimmering mirror over which the bright blue kingfishers skimmed and there was blessed silence apart from birdsong, the sky with barely a wispy white cloud to mar it, the light golden, the sun still low. I notice that swallows and swifts are just beginning to perch on the power line. Henceforth, day by day more birds will perch there and this means they are beginning to think of leaving this place and returning to Africa, but for now they skim the surface of the water cramming as many insects as they can down their beaks, fueling up for the long flight home. Now the geese are flying low over the Island in large formations, their rippling wing beats fill the air. They're Canada geese who have long forgotten how to fly to Canada but they go through their migratory motions twice daily here reminding me that Autumn is coming.

One time I sat on my front deck munching a bacon roll. Some of the river people drove off to work, but their departure was barely noticeable, for I noticed that swallows, swifts and martins were lining up with their new children on the power line and that was a message to me. It means the Summer will soon be over and Autumn and Winter will follow.

Then another morning as I sat on the front deck I witnessed the wonderful day when all the Africa bound birds came together and circled above me, parents with their young all anticipating the long flight back to Africa. There were thousands and thousands of them flying higher and then as if they heard some cosmic starter pistol they all headed off south and within minutes the sky was bereft of their elegant soaring diving forms and they were all gone. See you next Spring.

The Universe had put me there to witness their departure. This was my calendar. This was my newspaper – free, unbiased, devoid of adverts, celebrity bimbos and sports pages. How rich this connection has made me, rich enough to understand how rich those people from the past were also. I am therefore connected to them in a timeless way - a meditation during which I listen, watch and feel the messages the natural world is sending me. In this sacred space you can learn to feel the air, feel the day to come, feel the pulse of the natural living Universe, have dialogue with yourself and your connection with it and in doing this you can be aware that once everyone had this connection.

I read somewhere that anthropologists have discovered that 20,000 years ago human brains were bigger than they are today – the reason for this was that being nomadic hunter gatherers they often inhabited rivers and coastal regions where there was plenty of fish and sea food available. Having larger brains presumably means that our ancestors were more intelligent. You can't help but wonder what they did with the extra brain power – did they have abilities we've now lost? Perhaps they might have been telepathic, perhaps they were psychokinetic and were able to manipulate their environment by thought alone.

When we wonder at the architectural wonders of the ancient world it makes you think and we can remind ourselves that everything we do and achieve begins with thought. There is no way we can know what they thought about and what they could do but in my own small way I gradually sensed the echoes of those possibilities. How do animals know when to migrate, how can birds navigate enormous distances? They seem to know things that we've lost.

Usually, I had no idea what day, date or sometimes even which month it was. These divisions are imposed by 'civilization' like time itself, but I lived by a different clock – a natural timepiece that was whispered to me by the birds, the position of the sun and the moon, the temperature, the light, the weather, the river itself. I can't even begin to explain how wonderful this was – and how wasted a large portion of my life had been living by the other man-made clock. I'd been a slave to a tyrannical regime that had captured time itself. What else, what other freedoms had been stolen from us? A great many I discovered. The prisoner can only see that which shows through the bars of his cell, he is oblivious to what is beyond that narrow perspective. So much has been stolen from us, so much has been lost that we fail to see now. Today, we equate the word 'rich' with money but I've always believed that we can be rich in so many non-materialistic ways. I found my beliefs were confirmed.

At night I would lay in bed listening to the rain on the roof of the boat, warm, safe, sheltered, gently rocked by the water. My floating steel home became a cave, or an animal's burrow. I was more aware of the world outside somehow and that enhanced the real feelings that shelter evokes – safety, peace, protection from the dark and the elements. Thus, I was connected to the essence of what shelter means and in turn, everyone who ever sought shelter, found it and was grateful for it.

For much of my life just like many other people I woke up to the sound of an alarm, blearily gulped a cup of tea and flopped behind a steering wheel to begin a day unconnected. Those who are blessed to have a job that they have chosen that fulfils them are very rare. For most people the job they have to do is an ordeal and there may be little opportunity for fulfilment or pleasure. Most of the jobs I did were like that. Some were so intensely boring that they seemed like psychological torture, many were hard physical labour - but often it was in those jobs that I was privileged to work alongside the most wonderful people and even though the days and weeks were like serving a prison sentence of unknown length I learned far more than I would have in any university.

I've always had a problem with men. I'm a man myself yet I'd come to realise that right from my childhood I've never felt comfortable with them. This has been a problem in that I've never fitted in with them, always found them difficult to relate to and therefore I've had very few male friends. On the other hand, I've usually found women much easier to relate to and communicate with. The first half of my working life was spent in predominantly all male jobs, but in the latter half of my working life the opposite was true. I've thought about this a great deal and wondered why?

I've almost always found women to be far more interesting and communicative. That doesn't mean that I have an idolised view of women – far from it. Various women have caused me a great deal of grief in my life and I'm fully aware of how vicious, vindictive and even downright evil they can be. In the past the lives of men and women were demarcated by their physical roles – men hunted and defended and so they became naturally insular and isolated as individuals. I think it's true to say that every man is alone in a way that women never are. Every woman has a connection with other women that stems from their early roles. Isn't it tragic that men and women have this barrier between them?

Maybe it's because I had an ignorant brutal father that I hated and a mother who tried to dominate and control me that things turned out as they did for me. The truth is I love women, thoroughly enjoy their company and I've always been sexually attracted to them but I'd never want to be one. I've had the most fulfilling relationships with women yet I couldn't say that about any of my dealings with men. Men to me are often distant, isolated, barely able to communicate about anything relating to themselves and are usually disappointing to know. It's not surprising I've always felt isolated myself because I couldn't fit into the roles others expected of me.

I spent three years of my life as a taxi driver – which was probably the best educational experience I ever had because I experienced the human race at its best and at its worse – from drunken idiots on Saturday nights to parents bringing home their new born baby, from forlorn looking young men waiting with their few belongings stashed in a black bin liner because their relationships had broken down, to mature couples returning from an anniversary meal at a restaurant. I had the most intimate conversations with some passengers who seemed quite willing to talk about their personal lives with a stranger. I took people to hospital to visit dying partners, to cemeteries to mourn dead children, to airports for holidays, to job interviews – every aspect of every human situation was presented to me. For some of my colleagues these experiences coupled with the stress of driving made them angry and bitter, but for me it was a wonderful privilege that I learned so much from.

At one chapter of my life, I worked with disabled children in a respite unit. All of these children had the most heartbreaking challenges in their lives as did their parents - parents who were so exhausted by caring for their child that they brought them to the unit for a day or two's break. Often, they were single parents with other children to care for as well.

I will remember them all my life. In particular, the six-year-old girl who had so many birth defects her life consisted of one major operation after another – ironically many carried out by her own father who was a top surgeon. There were beautiful looking children with conditions like cerebral-palsy or extreme autism who had no connection with anyone or anything, who could not be left unattended for a second in case they would harm themselves or others.

The most horrifying of all were the two brothers who were both deaf and blind who spent their entire lives strapped securely in special wheelchairs trying to gouge out their own eyes. Some weekends the conditions of the children we had to care for were so impossibly destructive that the only thing we could do was to strap them in the minibus and drive them around for hours and hours. I'll never forget the smell of that bus.

Such experiences made me question the meaning of life itself. What is the sanctity of life for children so profoundly afflicted? How can anyone have an opinion about whether life should continue in the case of children like these? I can't. I found it hard to be around regular people in the outside world who had opinions but no conception of these things. How fortunate they were in their ignorance. Millions of people – nurses, doctors, police, prison workers, social workers, carers and the like who work with the extremities of humanity and human behaviour often for lousy pay would dearly appreciate being bored by their jobs, but they do those jobs heroically – at least until they can't face them any longer. It's what they do – until they are fortunate enough to find the opportunity, or the courage to disconnect from the madness that is modern life, yet fate – which I had always believed had been extremely unkind to me - guided me here to the Island and connected me. Could there be a greater kindness?

Why had I become so damaged, so worn out? There were many reasons which I won't go into here for this is not the place to revisit those dark places even if I chose to. Suffice to say fate had taken me to places and situations I could never have imagined I would be taken to. I had not deliberately sought those situations. I had not committed any crimes or knowingly done anything to deserve the things that had happened to me.

I now accept that it must have been my destiny to experience what I did. Perhaps it was my in-built drive to find out 'why' that somehow ensured I would be educated by those experiences.

That seemed a cruel place of learning the Universe enrolled me into and even now so many years later there are many of those dark classes I attended that still make no sense to me – but I learned, I learned about the depths of human existence the depravity, hopelessness and despair, the injustice and the insanity, the evil that inhabits our world and somehow, I survived. Perhaps the reason I survived was for me to pass on some of what I learned to you now.

*I am a man who has travelled and known the breath of far
dark kingdoms*

*Read pages that cannot be understood in gothic libraries of
empty shelves*

And their silent words tore at my innocence

*And I was mutilated, carved by poisoned knives and yet I
healed and was re-sharpened*

*There was a time when I thought my destiny was to bring alive
the wonder of the world*

To places where a billion frigid thoughts reside

*Twisted, fused, locked, entwined, imprisoned in a frozen tide
unstoppable it seems,*

*Yet my faith in some kind echo of redemption would not
abandon me*

Though at times I begged it to that I might also be frozen

*And here I stand upon this naked beach and watch for white
sails of deliverance*

*To crest the blue grey sphere of my uncertain wanderings A
ship to bear me home to some quiet haven where I might spin
dreams with some precious wide-eyed woman*

And share the treasure that lay buried beside

*So many graves and false imaginings the untarnished
wisdoms of eternity*

Poem - Les Richards

Repairs

After a year or two of my new life in my floating home it became necessary to carry out a major repair on my boat. Bou was leaking water through the stern gland – this is where the drive shaft from the engine passes through the rear of the hull to the propeller. There is normally a slow drip into the bilges of all boats since it's just about impossible to keep the water out 100%. Since Bou was around 30 years' old this was normal wear and tear and the drip was getting beyond the capabilities of the grease and the bearings to restrain it. And so Bou had to be craned out of the water into a boatyard to have this repaired but this also was an opportunity to have the hull blacked.

This meant I spent around two weeks living on my boat on dry land. The shaft was disconnected from the engine and gearbox and this revealed that it had a deep groove in its surface made by the felt washer it passed through – this was what was allowing the water through – quite amazing to think that a soft felt washer could wear its way through a hardened steel shaft. The shaft and the bearings needed replacing and in addition the propeller itself was in poor condition.

I found a wonderful engineering company based on an old airfield that renovated brass propellers and they also supplied a new length of shaft. I've always found engineering interesting and I was able to watch as a young engineer machined the length of gleaming steel to suit Bou's requirements, the correct taper on the shaft to fit the prop and the forming of a small 'trench' in the metal for what is known as a 'woodruff' key. This keeps the prop fixed to the shaft. When the prop was renovated, I was astounded – all the old gouges and corrosion had gone and it was now a golden vision of polished brass. Next the whole thing had to be put back in the boat, carefully lined up and everything tightened up securely. Then Bou was hoisted into the air and placed back in the water. What a relief to be floating again, to be able to travel freely upon the water.

During my time on the Island, I had Bou blacked maybe five times but not always in a dry dock. A couple of times the boaters from the Island got together with the boaters from another colony and hired a mobile crane. About fifteen boats were lifted out of the water and placed beside each other where they could be pressure washed and blacked over a two-week period. It was quite scary to watch Bou dangling from two canvas straps high in the air, but the crane operator knew his stuff. In fact, my big white cat Sandy was inside and never even stirred from his slumber.

This communal boat blacking was a wonderful event, an illustration of how communities can work together, share resources and knowledge and advice, a marvellous cooperative social opportunity. No one was in charge it seemed, but it all went harmoniously. The crane owner got paid for lifting the boats out, then for lifting them back in after two weeks and everyone was happy. Why can't the outside world operate in this way I wondered? In the past nomads probably got together to trade I imagine, friendships were made, connections formed, knowledge shared. I certainly learned from this gathering and in doing so caught those echoes from the past and savoured them.

When Bou first went into dry dock for blacking, I had her rudder extended which helped a great deal with steering. Blacking should be carried out every three years if you really want to keep your boat in shape. Steel will naturally rust unless it's got three layers of bitumen paint protecting it. So, every three years a trip to the boat yard and into a dry dock. The process takes about a week. It's a smelly, messy, dirty process and very disconcerting to be stuck out of the water cut off from the nomadic life. I soon realised that being temporarily deprived of the ability to move was like being a prisoner – yet all the time I'd lived on the land I hadn't had the vaguest idea that I was imprisoned. I could now understand that most people are prisoners by how and where they lived. It was another revelation to me. I understood that my short spell on the land was another analogy. My boat was repaired back to its healthy state. I myself was Like Bou - I wasn't being changed, I was being repaired, refurbished, put back to my natural state and believe me I really needed serious repairs and one of the most important truths I learned was that it's people who screw you up - but it's people who can heal you.

A child that's being abused by its parents doesn't stop loving its parents
  It stops loving itself

- Shahida Aribi

A different life in a different world meant different people and different relationships. There were people who you depended upon; mechanics, electricians' people who knew how to do the things you don't know about. These people were to be respected for who they are and not just what they could do. Then there were your neighbours – fellow boaters. Some of these were not so nomadic - in fact some never left their moorings, although I couldn't understand that myself. Why have a boat if you don't sail it? It's like having a car you never drive. Anyway, each to their own and everyone is different.

When I first went there the Island was inhabited by people with similar motivations to my own – escapees from the madness of the world. There were also a surprising number of retired people who didn't travel much but loved the Island life. There were some residents that I would describe as people who had been rejected by the world. Some of these people had been damaged emotionally as well as financially by divorce, trauma, and excessive stress. Some of them kept themselves to themselves, some involved themselves socially but they were all respected, tolerated and cared for.

We often commented that it would be almost impossible to come to harm on the Island because of the nature of the community - although out beyond the Island in soulless towns people were quite often chronically lonely, isolated and might lay dead for weeks, even months in a filthy flat before anyone noticed they were not around anymore.

As my time there passed the make-up of the Islanders changed a little. There were more lifestyle-choice younger people, couples who wanted a less materialistic life. Generally, there was a fairly regular turnover of people, some went to other moorings, some returned to the land, some met new partners and moved away, some died, just like any other community. The difference was that on the Island everyone knew about everyone else whereas in a town or a street you might be lucky to know only your nearest few neighbours.

Then there were the people you got to know more intimately – friends and lovers. Among these were those who visited me on my boat and my Island. Naturally people wanted to experience a trip on the river. Most of my friends were women – that was, as I've already said, because I'd spent the latter part of my working life in predominantly female work environments, but as you might imagine quite often these friends became more than friends and some stayed longer than others.

These relationships were eventually unsatisfying to me because many of the women I met seemed to regard the male-female unit as a kind of battlefield instead of a shared experience.

The scourge of feminism was to blame. Having lived through the period when 'Marxism in a dress' began the long march of Communism into every aspect of western society I was disheartened to find how pervasive this cancer had become for so many.

I was never a competitive person and I always regarded relationships to be a shared experience, unfortunately, there are always some who think they are more equal than others. Ultimately though a tribe can have only one leader and a boat can only have one Captain, someone who takes the ultimate responsibility.

Experience is the name everyone gives to their mistakes

-       Oscar Wilde

'Bou' was seventy feet long and so her bow stuck out further than the other boats moored near her on the Island. That meant the front deck provided an uninterrupted view of the river, having this different perspective served me well. It gave a feeling of detachment even though the boat was securely tied to the jetty. The bedroom was at the front so that was also a bonus in privacy and I could look out at the water even while lying in bed.

The front deck was the perfect place to sit and meditate, eat my meals or socialise. Coffee on the front deck? You bet. Sit and chat, watch the kingfishers in action, diving for fish then banging them on the boat before swallowing them whole, watching the fish swimming in the clear water, the swans, ducks and geese passing by, sometimes the occasional boat. Best of all in my humble opinion, was an evening sherry on the front deck – sometimes with a friend and neighbour.

My best friend and neighbour was a woman I'd previously had a relationship with. We met via the internet and messaged each other for some time before she decided she would like to visit me. Anyway, she arrived one Saturday morning intending to stay for just the day, but there was a birthday party on the island for one of the boaters and it was great fun. So much fun that she decided to stay the night and then decided to stay the next night. She was very taken with life on the Island and with Bou and me - and so we started a relationship.

This woman would come and spend weekends with me and of course I was naturally obliged to stay sometimes at her place – which was a gruelling drive along the roads and motorways of the outside world. After about a year of this I told her I was not happy. After all, I'd gone to live on the Island to get away from all that. She wanted to sell up her house, quit her job and move near to the Island, but she didn't have the bottle to actually do it. In a way I was not really helping her to make her mind up because while she was visiting me she wasn't making the changes in her life she really wanted to make.

And so, we parted – sort of. By that I mean we still kept in regular contact by phone and email. After some time, she finally did what she wanted to do – she sold up, quit her job, bought a boat and came to live on the Island. So, she became my neighbour, her boat being moored close - but not next to mine. Usually, I'm not one who keeps in touch or in any way lingers on the past, but she and I shared many years as friends and were there for each other through our individual ups and downs.

You don't get to choose how you're going to die or when – you can only choose how you're going to live now

-	Joan Baez

As for me I had quite a few relationships. Mostly these grew out of friendships. Bou was so long it really needed two people to manage her safely and I wasn't often short of willing crew but one resulted in the woman moving in with me. She was there for five years and ultimately, I'm afraid I had to evict her. Though we'd had many good times she insisted on filling my boat up with lots of unnecessary stuff.

Now I'm a very tolerant man – but it is a fault of mine that I'm far too tolerant for my own good. I put up with a great deal from her, but the final straw came when she told me I was playing one of my own songs wrong! No, I had been living with the wrong person.

However, I had the pleasure of meeting some very nice women while I lived on the boat. I'm remembering with a smile that once when I changed the mattress in the bedroom, I came across a half dozen different ear rings – none of them pairs. Maybe there's an analogy there.

You know I wonder how it is, in a world that pays us badly
Some people never lose their smile and they suffer fools like
me so gladly
Must be the way my friend that they learned how to love

Some people never let their pride become the master of their
virtue
Must be the way they're made inside, but they never knock you
or desert you
Must be the way my friend that they learned how to love

It isn't easy to forgive when you've had more than you signed
on for
But everybody gets their share I know that grieving ain't so
easy

But that's the way my friend that we learn how to love

Now you can ride a thousand miles, but you'll never find the answer
That's 'cause it's lying right beside all the ruin and disaster
But that's the place my friend where we learn how to love

Learn How to Love – Les Richards

Relationships are often a minefield that we have to blunder our way through since we don't have the natural capacity to find a mate as easily as the swans and other wild creatures do. Consequently, we make many mistakes and mistakes are usually painful. It's strange is it not, that birds and animals instinctively know who their mate is going to be. Some sea birds, for example, go off for half the year and come back to the same teeming colony on some sea swept rock and find their life long partner among millions of seemingly identical creatures. It amazes me that out of those thousands and thousands of penguins Mr and Mrs penguin can find each other. After all, they all look the same so why should it matter?

How is this possible? It's clear that modern humans have developed much more complicated and inefficient ways of finding a mate. I wonder if in the distant past we instinctively knew and recognised our life breeding partner? If we once did so then it's tragic that we've lost our ability to do this now.

Can this explain why there is this one thing we human beings ardently strive for yet so very rarely achieved without much sorrow and confusion, the one thing that preoccupies us throughout our lives, something that seems unreal, mythical, mystical, unobtainable - yet we somehow know it to exist even though it eludes our attempts to define it, explain it, to even name it. It inhabits the psychodrama of our most intimate thoughts and so often propels us on odysseys that drive the course of our lives. We call it love, which seems an insufficient term to encompass a multitude of feelings and emotions. I wonder whether our reluctance to really define these things is an indication of our grief at losing what we once instinctively knew? If this is so, then it is tragic. This thing is all but lost to us, yet we never cease to seek it – as if we somehow understand it is our human destiny to grasp and enfold it into our lives to restore us, to make us whole.

That this fundamental human connection has been removed from our consciousness is humanity's greatest tragedy. It incapacitates us to the extent that we may make many fundamental mistakes which lead to a serious impairment of our possibilities, our ultimate potential. It might even be regarded as a crime humanity has perpetrated upon itself. This feeling, this knowing presence haunts us from a time before history began, it calls to us across aeons, an almost forgotten dream, tenuous, yet enticing, something denied to us it seems, yet we know instinctively we deserve it. It motivates the artist, the writer, the philosopher, theologian, the seeker of lost wisdoms, it seems a thing of spirit unexplained by logic or science.

Once I knew a very wise woman who told me this true story. Back in the 1960's she and her partner went with another couple to India on tandem bicycles! It was, as you might imagine, a long and very interesting adventure. You would think it was a wonderful opportunity to learn a great deal. When they got to India the two couples went to see a Guru – and got an audience with him in his ashram. The woman of the other couple did nothing but complain to the Guru about her life and about the man who had pedalled with her all the way to India.

"He does this and he doesn't do that, he does that and he doesn't do this…" she whined, the list of complaints went on and on, but the Guru sat patiently listening to her ranting about her partner. When she finally finished complaining the Guru just looked at her and smiled and he simply said; "Learn how to love."

If only it was that simple. Maybe in the past it might have been – maybe it still is…but if you travel all that way and can't appreciate the person who helped get you there then you've learned nothing.

Don't hold on to the one who is leaving,
Otherwise, you won't meet the one who is coming

\-   C.G. Jung

People are not like swans or swallows; we can't mirror our moves and then get straight down to business. For one thing, the human sexes are not alike and they certainly don't look alike. A long, long, time ago apparently there was less of a difference between men and women, but there were changes brought about by the Earth's climate which brought our distant ancestors down from the trees and out onto the plains. There we became dependent on the wild herds much like I imagine the Native American plains tribes lived off the buffalo.

As *Homo Sapiens* developed the pregnancy period increased ensuring that the new born child was better developed, but that in turn made females more vulnerable and less able to provide for and defend themselves. The increase in a child's brain size caused the female pelvic girdle to widen, which in turn resulted in a widening of the hips and a shortening of the forearm. This meant that women became less effective at spear throwing necessary for hunting. You can see this when a woman runs – she holds her forearms up to clear her hips.

These physical changes brought about a general demarcation in roles. Men became largely responsible for hunting and women for gathering food (i.e. roots & berries) while predominantly involved with child care. Other changes resulted, for example; women lost their facial hair reinforcing the bond with their partners. Intercourse took place face to face strengthening the relationship, the female breasts swelling becoming in effect 'buttock mimics'. This one-to-one bonding brought about the essential compatible roles of men and women. Hunting called for better spatial perception and team cooperation predominantly in silence, whereas women's social skills and manual dexterity flourished.

It might be said that men had their focus on the horizon – from where threat or opportunity might manifest itself whilst women were focussed on the 'village' , the proximity of their children and the social interactions around them. Men tend to structure their social lives in terms of the hierarchies they learned or earned their place in the hunting party - whereas women were bound together by closer, family-based relationships. Men are far less likely to discuss their feelings or to admit to any weakness in the eyes of their male peers, whereas women generally feel free to share intimately their thoughts with each other. Even a man's body has considerably fewer nerve endings than a woman's so that he may cope better with injury or hardship. The roles of men as hunters and women as child carers and food gatherers – have defined the human species for the majority of its existence.

As can be seen the two sexes were physically, mentally and psychologically engineered by evolution to be a mutually supporting unit. Contrary to the dogma the social engineers now continuously ram down our throats, men and women have been designed and created by evolution over thousands of years to be compatible, mutually supportive halves of the whole. The futile attempts to change this incontrovertible fact are sinister to say the least. 'Equality', 'gender neutrality', homosexual evangelism and anti-heterosexual family propaganda is being forced upon us by political means to divide us and destroy our unity. It has contrived a war between men and women which must inevitably result in the destruction of both. We are becoming slaves to a New Order. Rather like cows, sheep and pigs the most useful, docile breeds will be genetically, psychologically and socially created and those who resist or do not fit the required parameters will inevitably be excluded from the 'farm'.

However, after so much change humanity still retains a memory of the identity it once possessed, for the enslavement and erosion of our true selves has taken place over a mere fraction of the time we have existed as a species. The elusive missing 'thing' we hunger for is still there in our genetic racial memory, it still calls to us and we should learn how to listen for it is vital for our own survival.

On the Island there were many women who had chosen to live individually, probably more than men in fact. There were also homosexual and lesbian couples. Everyone in the community got along just fine because this was a place where nobody had expectations of the way people ought to live. We were all there to get away from the toxic outside world, we were there to live as freely as we could, not the way the Government told us we should.

Of all tyrannies a tyranny sincerely exercised for the good of its victims may be the most oppressive. It may be better to live under robber Barons than under omnipotent moral busybodies…

\-   C.S. Lewis

Once, while I lived on the Island the Government tried to instigate a national census. The census officers were about as welcome on the Island as bailiffs or ex-wives. They couldn't get to grips with the fact that the Islanders wanted to remain anonymous - they did not want to be counted, categorised and transformed into data and statistics – they did not want to be domesticated. The census officers couldn't understand that the numbers on the letter boxes fixed to an old shipping container bore no connection to the boats themselves, and so there were hordes of frustrated, retired policemen and junior civil servants charging around with clipboards desperately trying to interrogate anyone they could find but getting nowhere.

Another time a local politician came along with a photographer thinking he might get some colourful background for his campaign by mingling with us alternative types. Both of them narrowly escaped a swimming lesson. Those of us who had chosen to opt out, naturally resented being pulled back in and of course there was no shortage of those on the outside who were disillusioned and stressed by the craziness. They were longing for a slice of freedom too. I called them pilgrims, unfortunately they rarely made progress.

People came to the Island, they looked lost, stressed, sometimes confused, sometimes they appeared hopeful. These pilgrims were on a quest - they were looking for a Holy Grail. They would stand looking at the boats, wondering – thinking 'should we risk speaking to that dodgy looking bloke?'

"Can I help you?" asked the dodgy looking bloke, smiling. They shuffled forward.

"Well, we were wondering…thinking about maybe getting a boat…what's it like?" they asked, relieved that I didn't attack them or tell them to sod off.

"Great," I said with a warm smile.

"Isn't it cold in the Winter?" they asked. AAARRRGHH!!! If I had a pound for every time I was asked that question! But being a bloke with an excess of patience I said instead;

"It is if you don't light the fire."

They smiled and looked relieved. The usual questions followed and I answered them. Will these pilgrims do it? Unlikely – but it's not surprising - they are just pilgrims after all. It takes a great deal of determination and you can tell that they are still in fantasy land. The world has gone crazy and getting crazier every day, but it's not so easy to get away from it all – though most people dream of doing so.

For many people even holidays are more stressful than the ordinary grind of life. Waiting in airports, spending more hard-earned money to give ourselves a 'break'. But what's the alternative? Isn't this how things are? It is, but not how they should be. Human beings were not designed to live that way, the natural way is profoundly different, infinitely better for us physically, mentally and psychologically - but have these pilgrims got what it takes to leave the madness behind?

"It's not for everybody," I told them, "It's a different world, a different life, but I love it," They seemed only slightly reassured. She held his arm, restraining him and looked disturbingly at the log splitter I was holding in one hand. To her I surely resembled a warrior from the Neolithic period.

"Is that your boat?" he asked, smiling, coveting Bou's colourful lines.

"Yes, that's mine," I answered. She looked at it and wondered - how many wardrobes there are in something that size and the terrifying possibility that soft furnishings may not be a priority on board.

"Do you actually live on it?" she asked, finding the concept impossible to imagine.

"I've lived on it for the last ten years," I told her, "Best thing I ever did," I added. He smiled. To him the concept was imaginable – if only in his fantasy. She was suspicious of his smile, it seemed to her that he had the potential to become uncontrollable – and that would not do at all. No doubt they would argue on their way home. These pilgrims had far to go. Chances were their paths might even diverge at some point in the future – but that too is a kind of progress.

A ship in a harbour is safe, but that is not what ships are built for

-       William Shedd

There were of course more single people living on the Island in boats than couples. As I've already pointed out a boat can only have one Captain. It's hard enough to co-exist with anyone else on a permanent basis - especially when space is limited. I found it more tolerable to encourage frequent rather than permanent companions. Having somebody else to share the magic with is vital, and I love the company of women. The truth is I didn't enjoy cruising the rivers alone at all. It seemed unnatural and downright wrong that I wasn't sharing wonderful times with another preferably female companion.

A shared experience naturally involves other shared experiences, intimacies for example. But my time alone on the Island when the boat was moored was precious too. After a lifetime of being cajoled or forced into situations I had no control over I gloried in having my autonomy. That's not to say that I didn't treasure the times I had with visiting crew persons and inevitably there were some who were treasured more than others. I treated them all with respect though. They were all looking for the right person, the other half of their soul just as I was. There was nothing wrong with seeking temporary comfort in the arms of another human being as long as you both didn't fool yourselves that what you'd found was anything more. We were all on a journey and didn't bear any grudge when it was time to explore further. There was nothing wrong with appreciating one's independence, freedom and time to enjoy being alone either. There's a somewhat crude saying that sums it up…

Sometimes the longest time of all is after you come and she goes

-       Unknown

A Journey to the Otherworld

I had my own pilgrimages to make and these invariably took me even further away from civilization. My favourite journey was the long trip to one of the nature reserves. It took the best part of a day to get there so an early start was always a good move no matter what time of year it was. The nature reserve is gradually expanding, for what were once vegetable fields have been landscaped to create a pseudo-Neolithic theme park world where the wildlife can thrive among wide reed beds and ponds. They have even introduced facsimile Neolithic animals like highland cattle to simulate extinct aurochs and obscure breeds of Russian horses.

This all seems very noble but like all schemes there exists behind them schemers whose intentions towards us human beings are not altogether benign for their plan is to expand these 'wildlands' and cram the people that are left into high rise smart cities. But let's not think of the machinations of the Globalists and their genocidal agendas for now – let's enjoy the opportunity to connect with nature while we can.

On the journey we travelled on three rivers – the one where the Island was, then the big wide main river, then we turned off down a long tributary. This last river was like entering another realm and the further upstream you went the wilder and more remote it became. At one point along this river was another splinter colony of boaters – the original pioneers of this colony came from the Island – they obviously wanted to be even further away from the madness. Onward upstream we chugged, passing some strange and bizarre boats moored at the sides of the twisting river. Wilder and wilder it got, further and further from civilization, the willows became taller and thicker. The marsh harriers circled high above, the terns dived at the silver fish that preceded our bows, swans elegantly glided past and watch the painted hull divide the water bubbling at the bow. It must have been like this for explorers on the Amazon, the Zambezi or the Mississippi.

Travelling at a heartbeat's pace time means nothing. You might even glimpse a small herd of deer in the undergrowth. Onward and onward, the wild riverbanks drooping willows resembling the primaeval jungle. Exotic birds flit through the trees – at least exotic by English standards – bitterns for example and high above big marsh harriers patrol. We pass through an overgrown wild area where the stones of an ancient moss-covered lock testify that once this river was used by barges to carry agricultural produce out to distant towns. It's all but reclaimed by nature now and the only traffic is passing nomads like me.

Eventually, as the afternoon is soon to become evening, we arrive at the nature reserve itself. The trees fall back beyond wide grassy flood plains contained by high banks, the sky expands. There are huge reed beds and ponds, there are swans in abundance and every other kind of water bird imaginable. There is absolutely no sign of human habitation, but there is a convenient place to moor up.

Here we have to bang mooring pins into the soft earth to tether the boat to the grassy bank to stop it from slipping back downstream. The current is lazy though and Bou sits snug against the shore, two planks go out front and back connecting us. The engine is switched off, the stern gland pumped and we relax and enjoy the wild spectacle. Bird song, booming bitterns, squawking geese, a soft breeze. A half mile beyond a stand of tall trees where it is said rare exotic birds called golden orioles call. I actually heard them once and called them back, imitating them, but alas I didn't see one. Across the reed beds numerous species of reed warblers warble and high above the marsh harriers circle and sky dance, lapwings perform dazzling aerobatics, grey herons flap around and if you're lucky you may see a flight of European cranes pass by. On the other side of the flood bank the former carrot fields now resemble a Neolithic panorama, wild grasses, ponds, reeds, highland cattle munching and if you're really quiet and careful you may see a herd of deer hunkered down. This section of river is very old and twisty. In fact, it used to flow in the opposite direction before the drainage schemes changed things around. It's hard to believe this is not a completely natural landscape but it is a facsimile, a re-imagining of Neolithic England.

The peace begins to sink in. You start to listen; to hear distant sounds, bird calls, the breeze in the reeds and almost beyond the human audio range the deep boom of the bitterns. The light is wonderful here and your senses feast and become more sensitive and appreciative the longer you stay. I would usually stay up to a week and in that time my mind and body return to the natural rhythms and in particular the sense of smell which is mostly redundant in the world we inhabit returns to something of what it used to be. We become like wild creatures again aware of every sight and sound and we begin to become aware of the messages from the past. It's a wonderful experience.

The mind should be like a pool of dark water untroubled by any ripple or wave which perfectly reflects everything around it like a mirror. Some swans fly over the pool and are reflected in every detail but after they pass nothing remains.

-     Taoist imagery

Living on the river you can become intimately acquainted with the rhythms of nature, the seasons and weather patterns, the trees and plants, the wildlife – all are in constant change and overseeing all these changes is the moon. If possible, I would try to synchronise my journeys to the nature reserve to coincide with a full moon. Most people now pay little attention to our beautiful silver satellite. Those that live on the land may hardly notice it above the brightly lit panoramas of their towns and cities, yet the moon has a profound influence upon the world and us human beings.

It's hard for us to imagine that until comparatively recently in human existence the moon was the only source of light at night and then only for a short period of our nights. That very fact affected everything we did, it limited our travel, our time available for useful work, all our night time activities were reliant upon the limited amount of moon light. If the skies were cloudy then even the bonus of a full harvest moon or a hunter's moon was denied to us. Our lives were divided by the darkness and the best we might do is huddle around a fire, a candle or an oil lamp, the great darkness outside a mystery, a place of danger - our world and our lives within it denied until the sun rose again.

Now that men have walked upon it, we know the moon as an airless globe of grey rock but once it was to us a place of mystery and magic. They viewed the moon as a triple female deity - the new moon the virgin, the full moon the birth mother and the waning moon the hag of death – the moon was a triple Goddess of Sky Earth and Underworld. As the Sky Goddess she was the moon in her three phases of New Moon, Full moon and waning moon. As the Goddess of the Earth, she was concerned with the three seasons of Spring, Summer and Winter: she brought life to trees and plants and ruled all living creatures. As Goddess of the Underworld, she related to birth, procreation and death. The remnants of this predominantly European belief system are deep rooted still in us. The powerful symbol of the mother-the bringer of life itself is hard wired into us.

The magnetic pull of the moon does much more than simply cause the oceans of the world to swill around and give us tides, it affects animals and plants and of course ourselves in many subtle ways – although we are often unaware. What really amazes me is that when you are out on the river somewhere nice and remote and the big orange moon rises up over the fens you can really experience that timeless magic. Once this was the brightest thing in the night sky and as such it meant you could actually travel at night.

There were other activities that the moon allowed us – the Harvest Moon - which meant the gatherers of the grain could work late into the night, the Hunter's Moon essential at the onset of Winter to lay in those vital supplies of meat, the full moon that marked the peak of the great green tide of new life, and the mid-summer moon that signified the equinox – the time of the longest day and the shortest night. The moon was a presence that looked down upon us, regulated and blessed our lives. So, if you can do it – get out on the river and find a quiet spot to moor up at full moon. Walk a short way and watch her rise and feel the power as the light brightens, see the landscape become painted with the moonlight, listen to the owls, the night birds, the deer, the foxes, the distant sounds of the night world and connect with those ancient, timeless feelings, that power, that mystery and magic.

For I have learned
To look upon nature, not as in the hour of thoughtless youth;
but hearing oftentimes
The still sad music of humanity, nor harsh or grating, though
of ample power
To chasten and subdue. And I have felt a presence that
disturbs me with the joy
Of elevated thoughts; a sense sublime, of something far more
inter-fused,

Whose dwelling is the light of setting suns, and the round ocean and the living air,

And the blue sky, and in the mind of man; A motion and a spirit that impels

All thinking things, objects of all thought, and rolls through all things.

Therefore, I am still a lover of the meadows and the woods,

And the mountains; and all that we behold from this green earth; of all the mighty world

Of eye and ear - both what they half create, and what perceive; well pleased to recognize

In nature and the language of the sense, the anchor of my purest thoughts, the nurse,

The guide, the guardian of my heart, and soul of all my moral being

\-   Lyrical Ballads - William Wordsworth

The journey is timeless, echoing countless journeys and migrations which now whisper to you across the vast plains of millennia. And now it's time to return to the Island. We could start out early or have an overnight stop on the way but the early start is best. It's just after dawn when everything is fresh and new and the wildlife is at its most prolific. We have to go a little further upstream where the river curves around in a wide sweep and we can turn Bou around to face downstream. It's shallow here at the edges but it takes a three or four-point turn. Then we're off, chugging through the drifting swans, passing the place we moored we say farewell until the next time. We will come again to this wild place where the past is strangely mixed with the present. We are indeed fortunate that this other-worldly place exists for us to learn from.

Remote as the Island is, returning to it is like suddenly finding yourself entering a busy city. It's ridiculous of course for you might only see a dozen or so people, but when you've had five or six days seeing no one at all it's quite an experience. It's like returning from a hunting trip. Everyone knows you've been to the far horizons and returned from the wild and there's a reconnection with the river village. This does not happen when you drive to a supermarket to get the week's shopping and your neighbours don't smile and wave to welcome you back. If only they did.

When you live in a small remote community you have to be a part of it – you cannot exclude yourself for everyone depends on everyone else to a degree. I remember one morning standing on the bridge over the channel at the entrance with a young man who had come to talk with me. It was around the time people were on their way to the car park to head off for work and thus most of the residents of one half of the Island passed by me while I was in conversation. I found myself saying good morning every few seconds and being wished the same by these people who greeted me by my name. It came home to me that everyone knew me by my name and I knew them by their names and there were a lot of people! I'd never experienced that before and I think few people do know the names of everyone in their community. In my experience of living in a regular street you're lucky if you know your immediate two or three neighbours and it's rare to actually know them by name.

That's a symptom of modern living – it isolates us, divides us, our house walls divide us, our garden fences, our individual privacy is now more important than our visibility and connection to those around us. On the Island you had privacy in your boat of course, but everything beyond it was common to all, there were no gardens, no fences, no barriers. It was a true community – like it was in the past when people had to share themselves in order to survive and that community was connected to the Waterworld

– more so I think than the other world – that world we had all rejected and escaped from.

The longer I lived apart from that world I used to inhabit I asked myself which one of these worlds is real? I could now understand that reality is not as concrete as we think it is. There is the reality of the 'normal' world in which most people exist but there are other realities like the world I was now in and that world too had another dimension – the connection to a world that existed thousands of years ago – and that place far back in time was there waiting to be rediscovered, waiting to be accessed – a place and a time to be experienced and to learn from – another reality.

What is the reality of time I wonder? In the Waterworld there were in the early Summer dancing insects (mayflies) that lived for just one day. Every living thing has its life span and thus each has its own version of reality. For us humans we might get to our eighties (or even further in these times) but for much of our history we would have been lucky to reach our thirties. What was reality like for those people who lived back then? Is it possible that there can exist a collective reality we can at least partially connect with? I think there is. To strive for that reality is to live free, to live naturally, to avoid the problems we get ensnared with when we live with all the complex distractions that imprison us today. The destination of that journey is to become complete and in harmony with ourselves and the Universe.

The human journey parallels the nomadic journey – both are journeys of discovery, both are seeking out the green pastures, the promised land, the ultimate destination. By rediscovering and understanding these insights, these messages from our distant past we can perhaps rediscover our true humanity, find a way through the insanity of the modern world and reach our true destiny. For some reason - I don't know why, I was in some small way aware of those messages. Perhaps it was my isolation as a child, perhaps it was just my fate but I've always wondered 'why', I've always tried to understand who and what we are, what our purpose is and why we exist.

Perhaps a way of answering these questions is to first learn about ourselves. We are far more than a physical body, more than our roles in life, our jobs or our family position. If we empty our pockets and remove our phones, keys, wallets and all those things we carry to identify ourselves then who are we? Man or woman, husband, wife, son, daughter may be a basic identification but we are all single individuals, sovereign over our own bodies and our minds – at least we should be.

What are we if we're not honest with ourselves? If we pretend to be what we are not just to conform with the outside world while inside we are resentful, angry and unhappy we are lying to ourselves, we are not giving those around us a true picture, we are living a lie. To live with this deceit will eventually corrode us and the time will inevitably come when our frustrations will burst out. I truly confess that I have been guilty of this deceit, but like all those whose lives are lies I had my reasons.

A woman who lived on a boat on the Island once told me that her husband had come home one day and said "I'm fed up with this boat, I'm fed up with my job and I'm fed up with you!" She was stunned because she'd had no indication he felt that way. Her husband left there and then – he'd run off with a young woman he'd met at work and she never saw him again. Sadly, she was probably the most bitter person I'd ever met – even living on the Island had not healed her, but I think her bitterness came more from her own guilt rather than her feelings of betrayal. Another case was of a man who had been married for about twenty years with a nice house, a good job and two teenage sons in college. One day totally out of the blue his wife left him. He'd had no indication that anything was wrong with their marriage and he was devastated for there was no other man involved – he didn't understand what had gone wrong. His wife simply could not pretend any longer. I suspect they'd both been fooling themselves.

The truth is that nothing is forever and we are fools to believe that anything is. We should remind ourselves that everything changes, night to day, the Earth turns, we are in the light for one time then in the darkness, the seasons change and so too does life. In the western world we have fooled ourselves that there is continuity, that the weather should conform to what we expect for the time the calendar divides up the year, that the seas and oceans comply with the forces laid out on the Beaufort scale, that if you conduct yourself in an honourable way then you can expect to be treated the same way, that if you eat well and exercise you'll remain healthy, but real life does not conform that way and neither does the natural world.

Somebody whose husband had contracted a terminal illness once said to me "We did everything right. Why should this happen to us?" What could I say? This woman had imagined that life was a contract with rules. She had believed that if she played by the rules life would do the same, but there are no contracts or rules in life. Sometimes the most decadent appalling people get away with murder and the most virtuous suffer appallingly. There is no cosmic judge to ensure fair play – we are given our lives to live and deal with as best we can. In other cultures, they acknowledge that life is cyclic, like the seasons and everything in nature. That's why there is a piece of Yin in Yang and vice versa, there is no way of knowing what is coming and no matter how righteously we might consider our lives to be we are all subject to the irrevocable rules of nature and nature doesn't do deals or sign contracts.

All there is will eventually balance out, but chaos itself is part of the harmony. We can only appreciate what comes our way, the joy and the suffering are inevitable. We are not immune from either. We are born naked with nothing and we will die taking nothing with us but ourselves for death is as inevitable as the sun setting and we might as well learn how to deal with the highs and lows of our lives, the ecstatic and the traumatic. In a few generations it will be as if we never existed. All of what we experience is a gift that we are here to learn from, our mistakes are lessons and only a fool refuses to learn from them – I know, I spent so much of my life as a fool and the best I can do is to strive to be less foolish when the time comes for it to end.

Man with his burning soul has but an hour of breath
To build a ship of truth in which his soul may sail –
Sail on the sea of death
For death takes toll of beauty, courage, youth
Of all but truth

-      John Masefield

Autumn

I had arrived at the Island in the Springtime – which was more by luck than judgement as it happened, but it meant I had the benefit of relatively pleasant weather and benign temperatures while I established myself and began to make the changes to my boat. I had some time to explore my new world a little, make friends, useful contacts and to learn and prepare myself for what would be the most challenging time of the year – the Winter. But before that of course there is Autumn.

This season has always been special to me for although Autumn is a time of dying and sleeping, the days getting shorter and the nights longer it is also a time of great beauty. It is also the time when the natural world can speak most clearly, for the turning of the Earth evokes the journeying in all people and all living things. This is the time when the Universe whispers in the ears of all living things that it's time to move, to head south to migrate, to shrink into the ground and await the Spring. The great tide of life is ebbing within the heartwood, withering the leaves, yet all around there is abundance, a ripening fruitfulness.

There is a harvest born within the shadow of the cold death to come that can help sustain the wild creatures and the seeds of the promised new life falling into the rich earth made fertile beneath the blanket of dead things resting upon it. Sweet chestnuts, acorns, whirling sycamores rain down within the bronze and yellowing coppery mansions of the forest. The green slowly disappears, frost-seared into flames of golden fires that cinder down upon russet carpets to cover anew with quilt-crinkled colorings - and in that bed of death new life will be born as surely as the sun will rise from the dark bed of night.

Death is something most people fear but for me I have no fear of it. Dying yes, I have fear of lingering painful illness of gradually losing my mind, my faculties, my ability to move independently, but I believe that when I die, I will become one with the Universe, my atoms will join the song of the cosmos, my soul will rise to eternity.

Now the bright sun lowers its curve across the sky and the colours sharpen, the air is hazed with a softening, clarifying dreaminess and the rich scent of fragrant decay pervades the senses, intoxicates the mind with soundless songs of eternal journeying and there comes a melancholy dimension for those who stay, an evocation of a vast primaeval longing perhaps that directs a need to bask in sun warm colours under bluer skies and to walk through the tall colonnades where yellow leaf-spiralling flakes entrance the eye, mesmerise the mind and soothe the soul with their ancient earthbound wisdoms, a balm for an unspoken grief, an echoed remembrance of a great loss.

Upon the running streams and still waters float vast, multi-coloured armadas, thin-curled copper sails painted with fire-patterned emblems, bound far away along rivers swollen rich with nutrients, yet crystal clear across dark round stones, buff pebbled shingle barred shimmering in the stream tumbles. Golden ships travelling dreaming waters, through spangled reflections, sluggish, turning, whirling slowly, pausing, waiting, until the rippled meandering current sweeps the myriad fleets onward, past the flood banked clay breached brown, past the spilled turfed and rich soiled branch tangling amid the wilderness twixt stream and the torn forest floor. Through root-tunnelled, dark-boled caverns beneath twisted trunks, sometimes paused against the fallen drift of twig and wind-cutting, tangled labyrinthine-textured, written on the wandering margined, yet ever journeying by the silvering stream-flow - and if one may stand bridged above the water, one may feel the power, the inevitability of the stream within one's body, the living force of its flowing, swift centred within its narrowing arms.

It is a time for copper coloured pumpkin moons to rise and glow the darkening blue-grey northeast skyscapes, to ascend and fill the sky with creamy luminosity into frost-spangled nights that part the veil of atmospheric translucence and reveal the wonder of the black eternity, naked, raw, bejewelled and unfathomed above - myriad far distant lights reflected twinkling in the flowing stream, their seemingly permanent existence reminds us that in death there is life and in life there is death. They are mirror-margined upon the pages of existence and should be read together. Death is but a journey that is on the other side of life, journeying hand in hand together, like leaf to stream, stream to river, onward ever onward to the breast of the grey ocean mother where the pure water of life will rise again.

Usually, the Autumn passed pretty quickly on the Island – or it seemed to. I think that's because almost all the surrounding trees were willows and the leaves don't change color dramatically, so one strong wind and all the trees are bare. It's a pity because if the English Autumn weather is mild you get an 'Indian Summer' where the multi-coloured leaves hang around a long time and there is the juxtaposition of the orange, reds and yellows against an intensified blue of the sky due to the lowering arc of the sun. I always found Indian Summers are extra dreamy and they can evoke a strong melancholy which can induce a pleasant trance-like state of mind. It's like a drug that causes you to rest, to sit and contemplate and wallow in a golden haze – at least that's how I felt, but perhaps I'd always been sensitive to it. I have no idea of the reason this happens, perhaps it's a kind of natural anaesthesia for creatures who fail to heed the migratory urge.

For me, the first Autumn passed without much time to contemplate it for I was busy adapting to my new life. I had thought that I would remain in contact with at least some aspects of my old life and maybe a few of the people I'd known, but day by day I found myself willingly leaving all thoughts and connections behind me. I was becoming fully immersed in my new life and there didn't seem any space for my old one. This might seem somewhat callous but I was now in a completely new world and the old one was as far away as a different planet. My whole consciousness seemed to have readjusted, but thinking about it, that was the way it had to be.

After all, I'd wanted a new life and the Universe had given me one for which I was very grateful, but there's a cautionary aspect to this – when you ask for something you are likely to get *exactly* what you ask for, but it might not always match up with your original expectations – so be precise and clear about what you're asking for. As it turned out I had no regrets, clearly the Universe had heard me and given me exactly what I needed. I'd put my trust and faith in the Universe and it had worked out well – how well I didn't know at the time I was simply grateful for what I'd received, but in time I would come to understand the true magnitude of those gifts.

Winter

Winter in nature is a time of culling the weak, it's a season of death for the old but for human beings who have learned over thousands of years to adjust to the cold by adopting fire, wearing thicker clothing, building shelters and devising strategies to store and preserve food it's survivable. It is the season when you really connect with the elemental. To those that live in the outer world it's a time for hurrying home head down, for staying inside, shutting out the wind, the weather, the cold. On the Island you were far more aware of the elements. You would survey the sky, the clouds, the colours, the way the wind bends the willows, ruffles the surface of the water. You could feel the changes.

The first frosts dusted the boat with ice crystals and transformed every tree and plant. The water became cloudy at times with sediment, soil pumped from the surrounding fields when they were inundated with rainfall. Only the hardy birds and animals remaining for the Winter is a killer, but this is the natural way of things. There are however, things that die for a good reason; germs, insects, some bacteria for example. If they are not killed off they will continue to infect and corrupt. I'm also thinking about unhelpful perceptions, bad habits, and toxic behaviour. Sometimes it takes a Winter to kill off these things a Winter of the soul you might call it.

This internalised Winter is not seasonal as in the natural world, this Winter can come at any time, it comes upon us when we find ourselves suffering from the mistakes we've made or the consequences of other people's actions. It might take the form of physical illness, the breakdown of relationships, the loss of employment, depression, or a recognition of being on the wrong path, going the wrong way and being unable to correct things.

These are cold dark times in the human experience yet just as there is a Winter in nature there is in the human journey, a Springtime too and a Summer. Day always follows night, but all too often we can drown in the dark times. Suffering is a part of life and although we may try to avoid it suffering is as inevitable as the turning of the Earth. How we deal with suffering is a challenge we all must face. We are born to experience life, to enjoy the good times and learn to deal with the not so good – this is the human journey we are all committed to until the journey ends.

What one person has to offer another is their own being – nothing more, nothing less.

-       Ram Dass

In our nomadic past we would have moved south to warmer pastures but when we became a static agricultural people the Winter was something to be feared and endured, I imagine. At the beginning of the Winter, they apparently built big fires and drove their cattle between them in a ceremony that they believed would help stop disease and sustain them through the death season.

Winter bonfires are still with us, the memory locked in our racial consciousness but now in England manifesting by coexisting with Guy Fawkes night.

I recall once at a pub I used to frequent in my misspent youth there were several old redundant lorry trailers stacked up out back in the yard and the Landlord gave us lads permission to burn them on Guy Fawkes night. The bases of these trailers were wood and pretty soon there was a blazing fire under them. Then a strange thing happened. Completely instinctively, somebody ran over the top of the burning trailers, others began to follow until there was around ten of fifteen young men fire dancing over them as the wood was being consumed. This was completely spontaneous, no one instigated the act - it just happened as though some ancient impulse had been ignited by the fire and the night. It was a weird and somewhat frightening experience to watch as the flames grew higher and the burning wood became less able to support the running men and you could see that inevitably somebody would get seriously burned. Eventually one man's boot went through the burning wood into the fire and fortunately he was able to quickly extract his foot and jump off the bonfire.

That ended the fire dance – but the ritual had happened as it perhaps did way back in the past. Maybe this incident was an echo of Samain - a festival usually celebrated on November 1st that marked the Celtic new year, the end of the harvest season and the start of Winter. The Celts believed that the veil between the living and the dead was very thin at this time. Nowadays this has also become associated with Halloween.

On the life journey there are dangerous places that might trap, or even kill a traveller. We can perhaps also view these places of opportunity, places we can learn from and even go forward revitalised. What if the bad things that happen to us could be gifts in disguise? To understand how this can come about takes transformation – the changing of one thing into another.

There is one transformation that is a vivid analogy of this – the diamond is the blackest, hardest thing on Earth when it is dug from the ground, it has been deep in the Earth subjected to colossal pressures and immense heat but once it is released from the darkest pit and carefully cut by the skilled blows of the diamond cutters chisel a shining jewel appears – still immensely tough but immensely beautiful.

We're like blocks of stone out of which the sculptor carves the forms of men.

The blows of His chisel which hurt us so much are what makes us perfect.

The suffering in the world is not the failure of God's love for us; It is that love in action,

For believe me this world that seems to us so substantial is no more than the shadowlands. Real life has not begun yet.

- C.S. Lewis in the 1990 play Shadowlands by William Nicholson

For me the Winter was something I had to be prepared for; collecting as much fuel for the range as I could, covering the boat's windows with plastic film – a cheap and effective double glazing, checking the engine and batteries are in good condition, laying in some extra tinned food in case the Island got cut off by snow or flood, and of course ensuring that we had extra gas bottles for the kitchen cooker and the hot water heater and filling the huge tank in the bows and keeping it topped up so that I had water no matter how thick the river froze. By preparing for Winter, I earned some security and, in my way, connected to the past. There was much satisfaction in this. The threat of the coming Winter was real enough to those of us who lived on the river and the frost upon Bou's roof urged me to heed its warning.

At the tail end of January, it was cold enough in the mornings for the first thin layer of ice to form on the water. When you wake up on such a morning you have to choose whether to stay under the quilt, or get up – but it's not really a choice, more of a dilemma. You see, if you don't get up and light the stove the boat will remain cold. So, you get up and do what must be done – then get back under the quilt until the kettles are singing and the cabin is warmed up enough for human habitation. Actually, it's quite nice to lie under the quilt listening to the flames roar and the iron of the stove ticking as it expands.

Outside the world is white-dusted with frost, but when the sun begins to rise we are treated to a spectacular show…blue mottled clouds tinge with pink-red glow, the golden sun-yellow near the horizon spreads until for a few truly stunning moments the sky becomes a display that transfixes you to stand and watch in awe. It's transformation – black freezing night into glorious day. Many people may be still hiding under their quilts while this wonder takes place – the blaze of glory that heralds a new day. Don't miss it – it's the dawn of the very first morning of the rest of your life.

When it snowed it was always a bit of a shock. Sometimes it came down sideways like a real blizzard for a while, but it didn't stop anyone from getting to work and it melted away in a couple of hours. Some Winters it covered everything for weeks and the water can freeze over which is tough for the wildlife and we were always aware of the wildlife there and we wished them well.

One Winter it snowed really bad and it got unusually cold, so cold that everything froze, the water beneath the boat froze to around two inches thick, the toilets in the toilet block froze and every tap froze - except the one tap that leaked. A leaking tap may be an annoyance in more clement times, but in the frozen white-out it was a godsend. Those boaters who were wise had filled their on-board water tanks before the freeze and prudently emptied their on-board toilets, but there are always those who totally ignore the weather warnings and so they found themselves in an unusual predicament. Water, water everywhere but not a drop to drink - it's all being frozen. But the Dunkirk spirit that lies dormant in all English people rose to the occasion. Selfless cooperation - which is always in abundance amongst the boaters blossomed. It was fun too.

The one unfrozen tap was connected to an unfrozen hose and a few nearby boats could be replenished. Frozen hoses - of which there were many - were taken inside the boats and warmed by their stoves until they could be connected. Soon an enormously long multi-coloured hose was employed to fill every boat. But Winter days are short and the boats were spread out around the Island so as darkness fell every hose had to be drained and taken inside lest it freeze again. The next day, the hoses were re-assembled and the operation continued. After three days every boat's water tank was filled. The toilets were still frozen however and so those who had not emptied their cassette toilets were in grave danger. Snow as we all know, blatantly shows full colour evidence of any unconventional sewerage discharge.

In addition, there was the problem of replenishing coal stocks to the far side of the Island. A sledge was made from an old surfboard and ropes attached to each end. One brave soul made the first crossing securing the rope to the far side so that bags of coal could be dragged across, the sledge was returned for the next bag. The ice being two inches thick supported the hero and thus the home fires were kept burning. How wonderful it is when people get together and meet a challenge in this way. Too many people now don't even speak to their next-door neighbours, such is the isolation and division that modern living has imposed on us.

In the Winter the starlings flock together and dance in what is known as a murmuration. The show began about sunset although on cloudy grey rainy days it was sometimes later or didn't happen at all - how do the birds know when it's sunset? Well, around late afternoon they gathered, flying in from all directions in multi-sized flocks from a dozen or so to hundreds to join the main bunch – how do they know which is the main bunch? These humble birds seem to cease to be individuals and become one composite being that seems to possess its own mind.

Us mere earthbound humans gathered near the reed beds to watch, sometimes bringing out chairs to sit and enjoy the display. The starlings started their dance right over the reed beds – did they know their audience was close by? How many? Impossible to say - many thousands for sure. The rustle of their wings is a sound you don't forget – soaring music in the air and the shapes that morph and form in the ballet surely must be planned?

Are there art director starlings, choreographer starlings? On cue individual formations split off and circle the main display, then return to join with the wheeling mass that dives at times headlong for the reeds, then rises, circles, weaves, choreography for certain - but who calls the moves? Poetry, synergy, ecstasy. Spectacular. Watching them against the golden glow of the western sky was pure magic. Then presumably when the collective mind of the starlings collectively decided they would, they all power dive into the reeds and settle for the night.

Naturally the Winter is a time to hunker down, keep warm and stay at the mooring – but there are plenty of days when the weather is calm enough to travel. Wind is the biggest deterrent; the cold doesn't matter so much as you can dress up to keep warm. I found that steel reinforced rigger boots that were fur lined were ideal for dealing with the mud and the outside chores – which in my case was mostly 'wooding'.

Keeping the stove going for long periods used an enormous amount of wood. I cut up all the dead wood I could find around the Island. Some enormous trees had been felled on a wild part of the Island as they had become dangerous so there was often the buzz of chainsaws when the boaters descended upon them. I never used a chainsaw myself – I consider them too dangerous as you only have to make one mistake and you'll have a serious injury. Living in a remote area you're not likely to get an ambulance quickly and if you're wooding on your own you could easily bleed to death. People on the Island had cause to appreciate the Air Ambulance helicopter when emergencies happened.

I was content to use a bow saw and even an axe at times, but most of the fuel I used was not 'tree wood' it was scrap wood which was dry and freely available from skips. Once cut up into lengths that would fit my generously sized firebox on my stove. I stored the wood stacked up in a construction made from old pallets. This wood store kept the wood dry and allowed air to circulate. The newest wood went in one end and the oldest and driest could be taken from the other end. Pretty soon the word got around that I wanted scrap wood and it was not unusual to find a heap left outside my boat from someone who was doing some alterations on their boat or in one of the wooden lodges that we shared the Island with.

Out on the Winter river it's a different world, the trees are bare but there is hardly any boat traffic which is a good thing because you can enjoy the wild world without the distraction of the dreaded tupperware. People who have narrow boats have to dress up like deep sea divers if they want to travel in the Winter because they have to stand at the back of their boats outside in the elements to steer - but that seemed ridiculous to me – why subject yourself to driving rain and freezing cold – not to mention blistering heat in the Summer?

Much to the shock of those traditional boaters I built a rear cabin for Bou. I designed a cabin that was the correct height to go under all the bridges on the system. I wanted it to blend in with Bou's lines but I wanted a fold down windscreen, doors on both sides that could be individually locked so that no one (including my big white cat) could inadvertently step off the wrong side and fall in the water. I quite fancied having quarter-light windows for ventilation and side windows that could be folded down in the Summertime. I installed a locking cat flap on each side which featured a fold down outside cover that doubled as a gangplank for Sandy my cat.

There was a company in a nearby village that made all kinds of custom machinery – mostly for farmers. You might think of them as modern-day blacksmiths. They were very helpful. I had to be careful about adding extra weight to the boat so apart from the lower sections which were steel sheets welded on to the existing hull the rest of the cabin was made of aluminium – mostly off-cuts that were laying around their workshop. I had to buy a new sheet of aluminium for the roof which I made in two parts, joined and sealed in the middle. Shatter proof glass went in the windscreen and rear windows but the fold down side windows were Perspex.

It took about a year all told to build but when it was finished and painted to match the rest of the boat it looked OK. In fact, it made Bou look a lot longer than she was. More to the point though it was very practical, it kept me dry, the heat from the engine below provided heat in the Winter as did simply leaving the internal door open so the inside heat could come through. I even fitted a windscreen wiper at one stage but I found it unnecessary because Bou didn't go fast enough to warrant the inclusion. A few of the traditional minded boaters found the cabin puzzling but I think everyone had to admit it looked like it had always been there.

Bou was unashamedly my boat and I had her my way. I did not need to conform to any other expectation or convention. This was quite a radical thing for me for I'd always kept my head down and been reluctant to show my true self to the world. Before it had always been too awkward to explain myself and easier to try to blend in as much as I could. This illustrates that I was living a lie – well I was - but sometimes the truth can be difficult for other people to understand – and if they don't understand they find it difficult to assess you.

Weighing it all up at the time it was better that I hid myself to a degree – after all my life got very strange at times and I thought it wise to try to fit in. For example, at one point in my life I was on the verge of fulfilling what was to me my wildest dream. I was working in a horrible factory at the time and I prudently did not tell any of my colleagues what was happening. As it happened it all fell through and I still had to go on working at the factory. Just imagine what it would have been like for me to have everyone know that things had failed. It's hard to live with failure, but even worse I think when you almost achieve success.

Failure is never quite so frightening as regret.

- From the movie 'The Dish' 2000. Quoted by Cliff Buxton played by Sam Neil

What is success anyway? I was never interested in making money, I never wanted any kind of career. I understood that what talents I had would never make me rich and wouldn't even realistically support me and so I took menial jobs that earned me enough to pay my way and had no responsibility attached. I'd witnessed people trying to 'brown nose' their way through their lives, pretending to like people whose association might benefit them materially – this seemed to me to be living a lie, being false and dishonest. I couldn't do it and so I used my artistic talents privately in my own 'secret' life. I sought genuine friends and relationships, but I soon learned these were not easy to find. The truth is it's hard to be true to yourself in the world we live in – there is so much fakery, dishonesty and counterfeit emotions, yet we yearn for genuineness, honesty and truth from people – should we really be surprised when we don't get these things when so many people live a lie?

In 2010 there was a study done in Germany about the energy we give out, what some people might recognize as vibrational frequencies – the feelings and intuitions we get when meeting someone for the first time. It's a kind of natural telepathy that helps us ascertain whether another person is safe or dangerous, friend or foe. The study - which was called SPANE measured the frequencies of those emotions we feel from each other – 'the validation of the scale of positive and negative experience'. The study imagined that anger or malice would be the strongest 'message' we broadcast out – or maybe even love - but in fact it is authenticity – what a surprise. Clearly, we really need to recognize authenticity.

As for me I had not been the authentic me for my entire life so far, but living on the Island had given me the courage to begin to be my true self. Everyone there was an individual, some more so than others but that was what made it so enriching. I was leaving the Winter of my life and finding a new honest me in the light of my new life.

This above all to thine own self be true,
And it must follow, as the night the day
Thou canst not be false to any man

-    Polonius in Hamlet Act1 Scene 3 William Shakespeare

Spring

After the challenges brought about by the Winter there would come the first signs of Spring and though the west wind still numbed the face and grey clouds showered the Island with rain and sleet there were days when the air was still, when the sun shone and the clouds were white floating convoys on the blue ocean, ships content to pass above us while the early flowers bloomed and the trees blossomed. Green leaves were beginning to color the bare wood stems.

Spring reminds us that the Earth turns, the cycles of life and death continue and there is always a time of renewal. I was affected by the Spring as I had never been before, the sights and sounds spoke to me and within me, the vibrant greens, the fresh bright flowers, the growth in the water itself, the plants producing oxygen that collected under the boat's flat bottom and burped and gurgled when any movement set it free to bubble to the surface. Life itself was blossoming, the cuckoo announcing the migrating birds were returning, a huge and benign tide of optimism and promise, a force to ride on.

In early Spring the ducks get randy. They have no concept of court ship, the males gang rape the females and even each other – they are not above drowning their rivals. Like the semi-domesticated geese that had imposed themselves on the Island they are not above killing each other or their offspring. The truly wild geese seem to behave impeccably though. I wonder if there's a message there? The collared doves never seemed to stop being randy whatever time of year and they've mastered the act of copulation on the thinnest of branches and even balanced on overhead wires. Soon there would be pike fodder ducklings – the female ducks are almost useless mothers, but strings of swan cygnets with their proud parents tour the boats, learning to tap on the hull, learning to scrounge, but I never so much gave them a breadcrumb. They are wild creatures and they have masses of natural food. It is miraculous that such noble, magnificent creatures grow simply from eating river weed and it seems sacrilegious to pollute their diet. Swans take enormous care over their young but wisely they chase off their offspring when they are mature enough. The adolescents live in large colonies much like teenage gangs where they eventually will find a mate of their own for life.

I sometimes witnessed two swans make love. An amazing and very moving spectacle. After some time mirroring each other's postures, the male held the female down underwater and then when they'd done the business their necks formed a perfect heart shape with their long necks. I would never have believed it had I not seen it with my own eyes. Later, they brought the cygnets around to show them off, gorgeous bundles of grey down with black plastic beaks whistling. New life everywhere - and then the swifts and martins arrived. These little birds fly from North Africa to reap a harvest of insects the thrived around the Island and to mate and breed. Watching the swallows skimming the surface, twisting impossibly to grab their flying food occupied me for hours.

Swifts are the fastest flying bird I'm told and when their young are hatched and have instinctively learned to fly their families screech around in impossible aerobatic displays. These birds seem to enjoy flying just for the sake of it.

And this our life, exempt from public haunt, finds
tongues in trees, books in the running brooks,
sermons in stones, and good in everything

'As You Like It' William Shakespeare

The river was especially renowned for its huge pike – the freshwater shark. They thrived among the boats on the island as the nutrients in the water attracted billions of fish of all kinds. When the water was clear you could watch their teeming shoals in the sunlight and some of the boaters would fish for pike and zanda – a European immigrant predator fish like the pike. Both are good to eat if you cook them correctly – some people claim they taste 'muddy' but they actually have a very pleasant subtle flavour and their big bones are easy to detach from the flesh. I was not a fisherman myself, but plenty of the Islanders were and the river had a reputation that brought in visitors with their rods. Some of the pike were massive monsters that had survived for years. There were plenty of eels too and invading American crayfish – neither of which I fancied myself, but some boaters put traps in the water for them. Once one of the boaters accidently ran over a wild deer and killed it but they brought it back, butchered it and distributed the meat between several people who had freezers. They even dried out the skin and prepared it. Now that really was like being in the Neolithic.

There were families of crested grebes – which are very attractive water fowl. They lived alongside us around the boats, carrying their striped young on their backs and teaching them to dive, swim underwater and catch fish for themselves. There were also otters with their cubs although you'd be lucky to see them – you'd be far more likely to hear them scampering over the boat in the early morning. Then there were the dawn choruses, usually instigated by the blackbirds. In my opinion the most beautiful bird song of all, intricate and dreamy. How is it that such a small creature is capable of composing music of this complexity?

On our own life journey the Springtime equates with childhood and youth – a time when we transition from being protected by our parents and gradually begin to discover the world beyond the narrow confines of our homes. When we first venture forth – usually to school - we meet different people with different parents from different backgrounds. It's a time when we make comparisons about ourselves and others, it's a time of great learning – how to make friends, how to coexist with others and we begin to learn what the outside world is like.

Then, after being fed a certain view of the world by the education system comes adolescence – an often-traumatic time between childhood and adulthood when our bodies change dramatically and our minds go into an often-tumultuous development. It's a time when we can be anti-social, belligerent and wild, we feel immortal and we do the craziest things. It's a time to experiment, take enormous risks. It's perfectly natural of course - our hormones are going wild and we sometimes make huge mistakes that can define the course of our lives. However, mistakes can be corrected when the time is right and the wrong turnings we may make on our journeys can be redirected. It takes the realisation that we've screwed up, the will to change things and the courage to admit we made the wrong choices and to take the journey of understanding as to why we went wrong.

The wrong choices are not always apparent. Not for the first time will someone choose the safe route, the advised way and heed the words of those who we think know better than us, but that too may turn out to be a disastrous choice for the safe, sensible way that seems to be the correct path, the path that most people choose will often deny us the wisdoms we could have learned through our errors. After all, if we never made mistakes then how would we ever learn?

Two roads diverged in a yellow wood,
And sorry I could not travel both
And be one traveller, long I stood
And looked down one as far as I could To
where it bent in the undergrowth;

Then took the other, just as fair,
And having perhaps the better claim
Because it was grassy and wanted wear;
Though as for that the passing there
Had worn them really about the same,

And both that morning equally lay,
In leaves no step had trodden black. Oh,
I kept the first for another day!
Yet knowing how way leads on to way,
I doubted if I should ever come back,
I shall be telling this with a sigh,
Somewhere ages and ages hence:
Two roads diverged in a wood, and I –
I took the one less travelled by, And
that has made all the difference.

The Road Not Taken - Robert Frost

I made a great many mistakes and trod many wrong paths that's for sure and I can see now that I kept on making more and more which just led me to even more and even greater disasters. It took a long time and a lot of grief before I began to learn from my mistakes – but I did learn and one of the big things I learned was that I had taken the wrong path. Consequently, I had no control over my life, I was dragged along by one crisis after another.

Ironically it was my fruitless efforts to control my life which had made this come about – if I had listened to the Universe – if I had known how to - things would have been different but I had ended up against a brick wall, I couldn't stop trying until I could try no more, until I put my fate into the hands of the Universe. That's when things started to change but it still took time. The wheels turn when the time is right, not when we want them to –

we have to be patient and accept that we still have more to learn. The wild creatures don't seem to have these problems, they are connected naturally to the Universe and they instinctively do things the right way. I had sixteen years living on the Island, sixteen years to adjust my mind and my body to a natural way of living, to grasp in a small way the echoes of the old ways. I was taken there by my own disastrous attempts to live in a world I was not fitted for, a world I could not fit into, but gradually I learned how to live.

The world breaks everyone and afterwards, some are stronger in the broken places

\-   Ernest Hemingway

I certainly wasn't the only one who had chaotically blundered my way through my life by any means. I came to see that for a great many of us our lives are not a pleasant journey of discovery that leads us eventually to harmony and truth, they are more often than not catalogues of disasters, each one forming the perfect basis for the next traumatic episode. In a world where there is so much knowledge available, why do we become so lost?

Becoming lost is a possibility on every journey especially when we don't have a map of the landscape we're travelling through. Yet there are maps that exist in our minds, much like the maps that exist in the minds of migrating birds and animals – they are natural and instinctual – the problem for us is, I think, that we have long ago meandered off the instinctual, natural track. Ceasing our nomadic ways and becoming fixed, static in the human landscape is it any wonder we've lost our perceptions of the nature of the life journey?

If we don't recognize the way anymore then it's inevitable that we'll stray into the unknown wilderness, the featureless desert, the dark forest where the tangled trees are so thick we are unable to see the stars or the sun, blind to the reference points that might guide us. We can easily become imprisoned in this 'land of lost tomorrows' – the place where we can't see our way through the undergrowth and it's often at the early stages of our lives that we become trapped - the time when we are raw and confused, when we have yet to acquire experience and the wisdom that comes from it. I was glad to leave it all behind me and continue onward and upward, seeking better things, learning more and more, enlightening myself, trying to understand this life journey, trying to avoid the traps and pitfalls. There was no way I wanted to remain frozen in time – life is a journey and if you don't take it you're going to stay frozen.

In these confusing times we now live in we are so far removed from the natural human journey that we don't just become lost and stuck in the period of adolescence, such is the magnitude and intensity of the dark forest that is all around us we can tragically remain stuck in that place – the space between childhood and adulthood. I look around and increasingly see people whose age might normally indicate that they are long out of the adolescent period of their lives, but who seem stuck in some sort of cultural time warp that has frozen them into the guises of punks, hippies, rebel bikers, born again bikers, mods, goths or whatever. Whole industries now exist to cater for this protracted adolescence – 60's, 70's, 80's events, tribute bands that are often better than the originals – and you can now buy all the clothes and accessories - even a scooter or retro style motorcycle.

Is this an indication that some people are reluctant to grow up – or are they simply trying to relive their wild, irresponsible youth? Are they experiencing a kind of permanent mid - life crisis? Personally, I have no urge to relive my youth. Mainly that time for me was confusing, hard to cope with and contained a great deal of destruction. I knew quite a few of my peers who lost their lives through suicide, drugs or accidents.

I guess they became victims of the dark forest, but it seems there are increasingly those who are still entangled in it. Are they still tied to the past which seems to them some kind of golden age, have they conveniently forgotten the heart aches, the acne and the confusion? Personally, I never had any inclination to return to the past – it seems to me like a step backwards when every step forwards is so hard won. I've always believed it's wise never to go back whether it's to a job or a person I've left behind.

Going back is to return to the wilderness and you'll inevitably repeat the situation that had you getting lost in the first place. If we are fortunate to be able to fight our way through this labyrinth we can emerge into the Springtime of our lives and grow straight and strong, we can proceed on our journey in the sunshine, on the clear path that is our rightful destiny.

Hard is the time in the wilderness years
Sailing oceans of pain, crossing deserts of tears
We wander, alone
Nothing is sure in the wilderness years
Nothing is known all is learning
And yearning for home
When we look back to the wilderness years
It's clear that this life is illusion
And confusion, made whole

Wilderness Years – Les Richards

Secret Lives

When I was at my primary school, I made a decision that sent me down a different path than perhaps I should have taken and this has been a source of regret to me in some ways, but in retrospect I think I was right to take that path. For one thing I know I couldn't have handled the consequences if I hadn't. In the late 1950's, every child had to take what was known as the 11-plus examination. Whether you passed this exam or not determined your future and really the entire course of your life. A pass meant you would go to what was then known as a 'Grammar School' which was for those who were above average intelligence and were more academically suited.

The alternative for those who failed was what was then known as the Secondary Modern School – which was there to mop up the rejects and train them to work in practical jobs. It might seem a sensible solution for the education of the young but it was a profoundly divisive approach. Britain in those times was still trying to build a socialist utopia – the truth about Communism hadn't really reached the west at that time.

I was expected by my teachers to go to the Grammar School but the down side was you couldn't leave school until you were getting towards 18 years old and for a boy in those days that meant conscription into the armed forces. The very thought of being forced into the Army terrified me. The initial training regime was brutal and it was not uncommon for conscripts to commit suicide. Even if you managed to survive the early period in all probability you would be transported far from home to help sustain what was left of the British Empire. I knew from boys who had older brothers how ghastly this was. There were plenty of wars going on in far flung countries that were fighting for their independence and there was the likelihood of being killed, injured or contracting diseases like malaria.

For me, an intelligent but insecure and isolated child, it was a terrifying time. I also thought it profoundly unfair that girls were not conscripted – only boys. So, it was when the time came for me to take the 11-plus exam I refused to take it. This caused a great deal of trouble because my teachers were certain that I would pass the exam and to their credit they wanted what they thought was the best for me. As for my concerns about conscription they couldn't visualise an 11 year-old boy even thinking about it. They told me I could take the exam and fail but that wasn't the point at all. It was unthinkable that a child should have the audacity to refuse the exam – I think I was the only child in the County to do so. And so, I went to the Secondary Modern school where I was even more of a square peg in a round hole.

For many years I had felt the need to express myself through painting and drawing. I think it was a means of escape when I was a child, but I developed some artistic talent which was recognized by the art teachers at school. In fact, my art teacher at my final year at school begged me to stay on, take exams and go to art school, but to be honest, I'd had more than enough of what passed for education by then and I wanted to go to work and earn some money. Also, I had very little confidence to do anything, let alone take an unfamiliar path. It was probably the biggest mistake of my life because it sent me on a path where I was forced to hide my true identity.

I moved through a different world where the people I met and worked with were in general poorly educated and had no interest in expanding their minds and so to fit into this world and with those people I interacted with I was forced to hide a great deal of myself simply because it made my life easier to do so. It had to be said though I wasn't always successful. How many times people looked at me without understanding, suspicious perhaps, certainly confused for we all like to put people in a box we can label and file away, friend or foe. It's a natural defence mechanism we employ until we get to know someone better and we can recalibrate the sparse information we get from others. I couldn't speak of many of the things I'd learned, I couldn't speak of my connection with the Universe, it would have been disastrous and so my journey was often lonely and frustrating.

It is important to have a secret, a premonition of things unknown.
It fills life with something impersonal, a numinosum
A man who has never experienced that has missed something important.
He must sense that he lives in a world which in some respects is mysterious;
That things happen and can be experienced which remain inexplicable;
That not everything that happens can be anticipated.
The unexpected and the incredible belong in this world
Only then is life whole.

-     C.G. Jung Memories Dreams and Reflections

I'd left school at 15 and I'd had no formal training. I couldn't really fulfil my expectations. However, music has always been an important aspect of my life. As far back as I can remember I had an affinity with music – it seemed to me a way of connection with the world beyond my own unhappy life and my soul reached out for it. At first, I composed music in my mind but I was frustrated that I did not know how to write it down, to preserve it. There was no one in my family who knew anything about music let alone how to write it down and in the early fifties the tape recorder had barely come into existence and was extremely rare.

In the 1950's music became more accessible with the rise of the record industry. Apart from classical music which was all but meaningless to me there was music in the movies. The 40's and 50's were a golden age for movies, a great time for film entertainment and for visual, dramatic and musical artistry. I found myself very connected to music and I listened to all I could. On the radio they didn't play much popular music at first but as the demand grew from young people and with advent of the 'off-shore pirate radio stations' all kinds of music burst forth and the record industry boomed. It was a wonderfully creative time for musicians, especially guitar players.

I didn't start to play guitar until I was about 19 years old – which is maybe later than young people begin these days. I was going to folk clubs then – there were plenty of them around and they were a good night out because you could hear not just folk music which was very popular then due to artists like Bob Dylan, Paul Simon, Donovan, Peter Paul and Mary but there were people who played blues, jazz and comedy songs. Folk clubs had a great ethos – you could see a really major performer as well as a complete novice and both were applauded and treated with respect. I was particularly impressed by those performers who had real charisma and could 'hold' an audience.

There were no videos to help you learn to play – you might get a copy of 'Bert Weedon's Play in a day' book which wasn't much use to be honest. At first, I didn't know anyone who could show me what to do either. My first second-hand guitar cost me £3 and being left-handed I was confused as to which way around I should play it. Left hand guitars were almost non-existent then. Anyway, I tried both ways but it took me a long time to settle with playing right-handed guitar. One night I heard a bang and the guitar which I kept under my bed decided to break itself in half.

Fortunately, I met a friend who loaned me a beautiful 'f' hole Hofner sunburst electric-acoustic he never used and I was able to progress – however the few people I subsequently met who played guitar were into playing twelve bar blues or rock n roll which I found intensely boring. Even the worst black blues players play far better and with more authority than any white man in my opinion. I was an Englishman with a connection to my English roots, not 'Blind Lemon Chitlin' from the Mississippi Delta. I persevered with what I thought was a finger style but it turned out to be a style unique to me. This was another thing that isolated me from my peers.

Unlike most of my peers I never wanted to be a performer – although I tried the experience both in folk clubs and in a band but I found it very uncomfortable – not only that, I found very little satisfaction in playing other people's songs. Writing and recording my own songs was what I really wanted to do. Then through a friend, I met a man who was a session musician and I learned a great deal from him. The first thing he taught me was how to listen to music. That was a revelation to me as I thought I had been listening – but as he demonstrated to me, I had just allowed the music to come at me. I had not learned how to really 'see' the sounds. To begin with music recording was undergoing a revolution and increasingly records were made in stereophonic sound which was not just the addition of an extra loudspeaker but was capable of projecting a more realistic 'sound image'. I learned how to 'see' with my ears in a way I hadn't done before.

I began to learn more about the art of sound recording and mixing the sounds together at the right levels. As the technology grew more magical it was possible to record four separate tracks, then eight, then sixteen and even twenty-four. This meant that music began to be created in the studio rather than the studio being merely a place to record existing musical groups and bands. It also meant you could create your own compositions by playing each instrument yourself (if you could) or at least do the basics and get other musicians in to play what you couldn't do yourself. As I learned more about playing guitar, writing songs, listening to the experts and recording in the studio my songs got much better.

However, my life lurched from one crisis to another and there was no time or space for me to really create the music I felt I had inside me. Then mercifully there came a time when there was a spell of relative normality and I promised myself I would buy my own digital recording machine and at last gather up the remnants of my musical endeavours and record them properly once and for all. I would do it all myself in my own way. I would not only be the composer and all the musicians; I would be my own producer and recording engineer. It was a big learning curve but I felt in control for the first time.

The unique guitar style I'd contrived leant a different dimension to my recordings. Thanks to multi-tracking I could blend the basic guitar tracks, doubling them up sometimes and more exciting using different guitar tunings and blending them with the regular tuning. Once these basic guitar tracks were separated out in the stereo mix they made an intricate tapestry of sounds which reminded me of the natural patterns of bird songs which can sometimes form complex rhythms. I also got a really good keyboard that had a full range of sounds built into it and this enabled me to add different strings, bass, brass and other useful instruments and sounds to my recordings. Before too long I'd produced my first album on CD. I'd even designed and printed the labels and insert cards and purely through word of mouth I began to actually sell copies. A few other collections followed, but by then I'd decided to sell up and go and live on the boat on the Island.

On the Island my life was not so secret – some of it I could reveal without fear or ridicule, but there are – as I had discovered perhaps 20 or so years before I moved there, secrets that are not secret. We don't know about them because we don't look, no one tells us about them so we don't ask. They are like the proposed massive housing estate for illegal immigrants, or the new by-pass that will be built right next to or right through your back garden – the plans are all 'freely accessible' on a dusty shelf behind a filing cabinet in the basement of the planning department, or hidden in a maze of small print legalese in the Local Authority's ten-year plan for development – which you won't even be aware of either.

These are plans that nobody democratically voted for, imposed by un-elected committees that exist in remote International Organizations that you were never consulted who will dictate how your lives will be. They are political agendas that are not deemed suitable for the peasants like you to understand or have any say in, yet your local authority and your national government have signed up to them and they will change your life and your children's future whether you agree with them or not and if you don't like what's coming then tough titty – you should have looked – the plans were there, you *were* consulted.

Some tenacious people did look behind the filing cabinets, they did read the small print and they did ask questions, motivated like I had been by events and situations in their own personal circumstances and they were shocked and horrified by their discoveries. However, when these obstinate investigators attempted to inform the credulous, trusting, beleaguered populace around them their warnings were naively dismissed as conspiracy theories and their dire predictions went unheeded. Sadly, there were quite a few people on the Island who didn't look, didn't question – although some were very aware. Those of us who knew about these H.G. Wellsian 'things to come' could often feel that they were living secret lives, but as I settled in to life on the Island I had found my place, found an identity that was easier to share among the other castaways.

There I was connecting like never before with the distant past, beginning to relate it to the world of now and even imagining that these connections might be relevant for the future – all our futures, but I was surrounded even there by many who could not visualise or understand where the outside world was heading. For myself I had an understanding of where things were going and my exile on the Island provided an escape to a degree, but I could not really feel secure for I knew what was coming – I didn't know for sure the form it would take but I kept myself well informed by the Internet, I continued to research and read widely. Knowledge is power of course – it enables you to make decisions. I'd imagined I'd done the best I could by living off grid, as far from a town or a city as I could, but England is itself a small island. When the dark tide began to envelop the world, I knew I could only be partly immune at best.

At the time I had escaped there were very few places you could escape to, but on the Island the people were refugees from the 'civilised' world like me – the one that is steadily becoming more intrusive, abusive and destructive, the world where even the most optimistic and resilient are becoming aware there is something terribly wrong. Some people choose to ignore what is happening and blindly follow what the current 'high priests' are ordering them to do, but their ignorance of what is happening is certainly not bliss and if you continually follow blindly you are eventually going to fall down a very deep and dark hole.

I myself could see that I was guilty of getting myself into bad situations, but it seemed to me that the whole of humanity was getting into an extremely dangerous situation. Things were happening on such an enormous scale that we as individuals seemed to be powerless to change anything. Yet, on the other hand I knew there was hope for change – after all we as individuals have the capacity for change – perhaps the whole world has the same chance? I began to think about this possibility – if we as individuals could be transformed by connecting in some small way to the distant, pre-agricultural past could there be a way of humanity achieving a mass transformation that would derail the course of destruction we were currently headed for?

There seems to be no way to stop this descent into Armageddon. Not only are we threatened by the machinations of Globalist dictators who want to imprison us in digital concentration camps, we are being harmed by the very food we eat, the medicines that are forced upon us, our natural physiological rhythms are increasingly devastated by excessive noise, artificial light and the destruction of the natural seasonal changes brought about by modern living. Those people who live in towns and cities are now relatively unaware of the cycle of the seasons. Most homes are centrally heated and brightly lit, people even wear roughly the same amount of clothing all year round because they travel by car, but our bodies and subconscious minds are naturally aware of the fluctuations of the seasons, the length of day and night, the amount of sunshine and the phases of the moon. When we are deprived of the legitimacy of these natural connections it's no surprise we get problems.

Having worked extensively in mental health I soon reached the conclusion that it was not that people as a whole who were going crazy – it was the world itself had become crazy. Now, how many people get to live on an island when it is the very thing they need? Proof again that the benevolent Universe was providing for me. Perhaps it always was and I had never realised it, perhaps it can do so for everyone and it's just that we don't see it. That is a profound thought. Imagine that there is a solution to all our problems if only we had the insight and the courage to recognize and act upon it.

So many of us are imprisoned as I was by the same ways of thinking, the same lack of courage, even the same belief that there is no other place, no other way to live – but there is. Whatever it was that has imprisoned us personally; childhood abuse, traumatic experiences, toxic parenting, whatever it was we have to have the courage to look through a window, to find our own particular Island, our own kind of refuge from the madness. It may seem impossible but it's not. I believe it's essential for survival especially in the world that has now come to be.

How do you find your own Island, your own Refuge? Everyone must take their own journey and find their own place. It may be a different place to live, a different job, a different understanding of your life. How many people spend hours escaping reality by watching movies or playing games? Fantasy is not reality – it's just a brief interlude from reality. It won't solve your problems or the world's problems – but, what if you could make your fantasies, your dreams, your innermost longings come true? What if you could be transformed?

How exciting it could be if we all might leave our castles, towers and our prisons behind us and rediscover the world beyond them, the world that existed before they were constructed. That world is really out there – you just need to find a window to see that it truly exists. That window might be found by chance or by some unusual or even traumatic turn of events that forces us to change direction. Perhaps, it's like being lost in a maze or labyrinth. Perhaps we blunder our way through dark passages and become lost – but it is by being lost that we find an alternative path. It's by being lost in the desert, or the dark forest that we find our way to the true path and the green pastures beyond.

We humans have been around for something like two million years, but it's only a mere ten thousand years ago that we discovered agriculture and began to settle in one place, so throughout the vast majority of that huge amount of time we've been around we were wanderers, we were all nomads following wild herds much like the Lapps of Scandinavia or the plains Indians in North America. The nomad takes only what can be easily carried, only that which is essential. The nomad understands that superfluous things will slow us down, burden us, tie us to a spot so we cannot move. Anyone who has ever hiked with a rucksack knows that the more you have to carry the more tired you become and more to the point is if you are thinking about the weight on your back you're not thinking about anything else and your mind is closed to what may be going on around you, the magnificent countryside becomes a trial, an ordeal to be conquered, you have no appetite to read the messages the Universe is broadcasting, no energy to meditate on the journey.

I'm reminded of the Biblical story that tells us that it is as easy for a rich man to enter the Kingdom of Heaven as it is for him to pass through the eye of a needle. I never understood this until I learned that the 'eye of the needle' wasn't a sewing needle, it was the name given to the narrow doorway that stood beside the main gate of a city. Naturally, a rich merchant with all his stuff on his camel could not enter through this narrow doorway. The plain facts are we come into this world without anything and we will surely leave it the same way and the less we clutter up our lives in between with stuff the better. The natural animal lives its life without stuff. Human beings actually needed very little to survive, but can anyone now imagine how the now extinct native Tasmanians managed with only THREE items of technology, or the original Australian aborigines with just five? Today we require thousands of things simply to maintain our existence – is it any wonder we are overburdened and unable to move forwards? Or can we do exactly that?

Before we can begin a new journey of discovery, what we really need to do is dump all the stuff in our minds that we don't need – the stuff that holds us back, the stuff that can destroy us. It always amazes me that when people get physically ill they automatically consult a doctor, yet when they suffer an emotional crisis or a traumatic experience they rarely consult a trained professional. Not only that it seems that some people are all too willing to part with their money for all manner of untrained, unqualified New Age quackery rather than invest in their own future well-being with the guidance of a well- trained experienced therapist.

There is a widespread perception that therapy is where neurotic over privileged females go to spend hours and hours talking with other neurotic over privileged females about the minutiae of their baseless over privileged lives when their time and money would be better spent on pulling themselves together, 'getting a grip' and getting on with the practical reality of their lives. I can understand why many people think this. The truth is that most of these 'professionals' are even more screwed up than the people who seek help from them and that is no help to the many people who find themselves devastated by the most appalling situations in their lives.

People who are in severe crises are faced with little or no alternatives to solving their problems. If they're lucky they may have a loving, supportive family they can turn to, or trusted friends who will listen and support, but for most people in desperate situations it's a visit to the GP who has no time to help them and so he quickly prescribes anti-depressant drugs which gets them out of the surgery double quick, makes a great deal of money for the multi-national pharmaceutical industry and will hopefully tranquilise them enough so that they don't commit suicide – which is another sadly frequent option. Alternatively, for those who wouldn't be seen dead even considering seeing a counsellor or a therapist there is the alcohol or illegal drugs option – which sadly often leads them back to the previous terminal option.

Where is the humanity in this appalling state of affairs? Nowhere – there isn't any, real humanity has been purged from the scene. In the past when an extended family was around for advice and support another wise and sympathetic person was usually available. Most of us now do not have the wonderful support of an extended family living close by us. The extended family was a wonderful treasure house of wisdom and advice but today all too often those families that haven't yet been torn apart live great distances apart. Neither do we live in real communities any longer. To be a part of and to take part in a real community means a person is known and knows others. In other words, the community monitors its members who know who they can count on for help if they need it. In the past there was usually a priest or spiritual adviser of some kind in the tribe or community, but in the age we inhabit there are very few places we can turn to – which is an even greater tragedy because there have never been so many desperate, traumatised, abused and wounded casualties of modern living.

So, it seems to me the first part of the journey is into the territory of ourselves. If we can rebalance our own lives, solve our own problems then maybe we'll be better equipped to deal with the bigger problems that we are going to be faced with. Do you think this is impossible? I don't believe that's the case. The knowledge we need is out there, but it's not going to be found in the prison we live in. We first have to get off our arses and go look for it. You'll find it in books or on the internet – which is the great combined mind of humankind and still relatively free for the time being. All you need to know is there - and like the plans for Global tyranny you just have to go look for it.

Who looks outside, dreams. Who looks inside, wakes

-      C.G. Jung

Abraham Maslow was a famous and very influential American psychologist who created what has become known as Maslow's hierarchy of needs – a theory that describes our psychological health in terms of the priority of our human needs. Interestingly, and perhaps appropriately in the light of my own reflections, he developed this theory in 1938 after conversations with the Native American Blackfoot people who had fled into Canada after their virtual extermination by the influx of people from Europe in the late 19th century. The Blackfoot were coincidentally one of the former nomadic plains tribes like the Sioux. Maslow illustrated his theory using a diagram of a pyramid which it is said was inspired by the shape of the Blackfoot Tipi tents. The pyramid is formed by built up layers, the most basic needs for life at the bottom; food clothing, shelter – safety and security, then being loved and belonging, friendship. Next comes esteem, respect, self- worth then up to the highest level in the hierarchy of needs which is self-actualisation, transcendence – the connection of the self with the wider Universe.

In his quest to understand why people became mentally ill Maslow decided that it might be a good idea to study what made people mentally *well*. It seems obvious when you think about it - but up until Maslow's work no one had *thought about it* that way. What was fascinating about his study was that all the people who he found to be mentally well – that is stable, happy, content and successful in their personal lives - had experienced what he described as 'peak experiences'. These he defined as incidents of an altered state of consciousness characterised by euphoria which were often achieved by who he called *self-actualizing* individuals. These were people who at various times in their lives had experienced periods of deeply moving exhilarating, elevating, ecstatic feelings that generated an advanced form of perceiving reality. These sometimes exciting, mystical experiences create the moment of reaching the full potential of a person's existence.

The true value of a human being is determined primarily by the measure and the sense in which he has attained liberation from the self
-       Albert Einstein

It appears that by rejecting the spiritual in our lives we are unbalanced, disconnected. Because we are not just physical and mental beings, we have a third component that we once had ready access to – our connection to the greater Universe – the very thing I've been discovering, the very thing I've been talking about here in this book. We are a Trinity. This is what we've forgotten, but it must follow that by reclaiming our connection we can become whole and balanced again – and who knows where that could take us?

When life brings us great challenges, we have no way to understand them or how to cope with them unless we can refer to the spiritual aspect of ourselves. In the west we've been subjected to 2000 years of Christianity – but the carpenter from Nazareth surely never meant for his teachings to be used as a method of social control - yet for better or worse that's what happened. The Council of Nicaea was convened by the Roman Emperor Constantine in Turkey in the year 325 *after* Jesus Christ's death. Basically, it was a get together of the elites who ruled Europe to define the new religion with the purpose of controlling their subjects from before birth to after death. It was the council that decided who was Divine, how the Bible was constructed and what was to be the governing methods of how the masses lived their lives. Whether that was a good thing or not is debatable. It seems ironic when you consider that Jesus Himself suggested that Christians should be 'as invisible as salt which nevertheless gives food its flavour' or 'as unobstructed as yeast which nevertheless leaven the loaf.'

Other religions operate in their own ways with their own man-made deities and their own enforced ways of control, but to me it seems that when God was named and defined the true Universal Spirit and its relationship with humanity was denied to people. Once everyone had a personal individual spiritual connection with the Universe – as all the world's creatures appear to have. Religion rendered that personal connection redundant and it outlawed the true nature of human existence. We are not just physical and intellectual beings – we are a Trinity that embraces the spiritual – or we should be. Religion removes our individual, natural spiritual connection. Religion tells us who God is and how we should live but those are the rules set down by powerful governing men. Consequently, we are out of balance, our equilibrium is destroyed so that we can be controlled, used and exploited.

Less than 10% of the population of the entire Earth has any knowledge or spiritual wisdom of what we know to be true

- Elvis Presley – written in his own hand on a piece of paper inserted into his copy of 'The Prophet' at page 63 where Kahlil Gibran wrote about death.

I spent a sizeable portion of my life working in mental health care settings which was at times very rewarding in that I helped people with problems overcome them, however, I was disappointed to discover that many 'professionals' - doctors and psychiatrists - were enslaved by the pharmaceutical industry and how opposed they were to what amounted to basic common sense and the wealth of knowledge and human experience that exists beyond their white-coat academic world. Tragically, this mind-set results in many people repeating their patterns of negative behaviour and often turning to alcohol or drugs to 'deal with' their problems. It seems as if there is a huge blind spot – a chasm that is for some reason now empty, yet once existed to support, inform and guide us through the labyrinth of confusion we all face in our lives.

During my own training – which comprised of three years of intensive work and study – not to mention considerable financial investment - I was introduced to various approaches to emotional and mental health issues like psycho-synthesis, trans-personal psychology and a whole range of counselling methods which are very effective – in fact I was surprised how simple it can be to overcome many of the problems we face in our emotional lives, yet the techniques and strategies I learned about are rarely in use and when I went to work in mental health settings the normal approach was pharmaceutical. Obviously, this makes a great deal of money for the drug companies but it does not help the vast majority of people whose problems can be cured comparatively easily, cheaply and quickly. You can't help but come to the conclusion that the government wants it this way.

It's money that drives all this – it's a conspiracy between governments and the immensely powerful pharmaceutical industry. Those that rule us want us to be mentally ill, want us to be confused, stressed and helpless, they drug young boys for behaving like boys. In a radically feminist education system where the vast majority of teachers are women with Marxist leanings boys are barely tolerated, they are actually taught that it is their fault as males for all society's ills. I've worked in schools. I've seen how boys are marginalised and I can understand why they want nothing to do with 'education' and are losing all loyalty and adherence to the society they are growing up in.

Marxism is preached in all our colleges and universities by lecturers who were infected by it during their own education. In my own lifetime I've witnessed the 'long march into the institutions' that began in the mid 1960's. Back then it was the Soviet Union who was funding the promotion of Marxism throughout western countries – initially through the popular student demonstration craze at the time.

In the UK this culminated with a particularly violent protest outside the American Embassy in London which was not successful from the Marxists point of view. Their next and very successful method of attack was to infiltrate and take over the women's movement - in particular through the Domestic Violence industry which was a ready cash-cow for them. From there it was an easy jump into the Social Services and Education system which was almost exclusively made up of university 'educated' women. It took a few years but eventually Marxism took over the Civil Service and the various branches of government so that now there is almost no difference between the political parties.

Consequently, Democracy is now dead in the UK and the western world. It was a very effective strategy for it drove a huge wedge between the basic male/female unit of society, the very foundation of the nation. It was a strategy that tore apart the basic binary form of the human species.

Whether you are politically minded or not we must acknowledge that it's politics that runs the world. You may try to ignore that fact, but unfortunately that is how most people are controlled. It is only religion that has a secondary hold over people's lives and that too is increasingly subject to political control. It is the erasure of religion in the western nations that has brought about the lack of cohesion and national identity which has made them an easy conquest for Global Marxism.

I wonder what you believe? For me I've always believed in the spirit of the Universe – which you may call God if you've a mind to and I've always felt connection through the natural world. That has been my spirituality. I need no church or Bible, no scripture other than what I see and feel. I have had no need for structured religion with its dogmatic conventions. God has been with me always - I never knew a time when He wasn't there. I think that the most profound problem with modern humanity is that most people have lost their connection, lost their spiritual relationship with the Universe and that makes us unbalanced and vulnerable.

However, sometimes if we are fortunate, the Universe connects with us. This intervention may happen when we are in dire situations - when we are so lost in the darkness that we can see know way out of our personal pit of despair. Something will happen to help us, it may be unrecognised initially, we may only see the intervention in retrospect, but when we examine the particular incident, we might see it as a message that the Universe is telling us that we are going to be alright eventually, that we are being taken care of even though the solution may take a little time to resolve. After all, we are as individuals just small cogs in the cosmic wheels and we should be patient and trust that those wheels have a great many cogs to line up. My own tragedy was that I had always been connected but I had lived in a world of disconnection – it was a terribly lonely place, a living hell at times where my very soul bled for release, but it was only after a whole lifetime of disasters that I found the Island, the place away from the madness where I could live with my secret unmasked and be freely connected.

Something in you dies when you bear the unbearable –
And it is only in that dark night of the soul that you are prepared
To see as God sees and to love as God loves

\-   Ram Dass

Retroperspectives

My semi-nomadic life seemed to indicate to me there was a possibility that we could learn from our past in a similar way that I personally had discovered. We might somehow craft a different future than the one that is being imposed upon us. I had escaped my own slavery and found a measure of freedom just as many others have done, but is this possible for the rest of humanity?

Can we somehow disconnect from the present form of slavery and reconnect with the natural world and with it the greater, wider Universe? Only therein I think lies our true destiny and the ultimate purpose of the human species. Somehow, we might learn how to free ourselves from the dark forests and take our rightful path. Where will that path lead us to - the stars - or to oblivion?

We don't have to become hermits or wandering vagrants and we certainly don't have to give up the wonderful benefits that technology has brought into our lives. Maybe what we can do is learn from our past journeying to take the right turning, to avoid the dangerous precipice, to conserve our strength for the uphill climb, to take advantage of the rich grazing so we might survive the desert. Perhaps we can learn to see in our minds the map we once had.

Perhaps we can reconstruct that map. With it we can stick to the track, attempt to live honourably, avoid the excess, the unnecessary, and the superfluous – we can live without waste crimes as well as war crimes. Then, what we can do in our own way is to explore and enjoy the echoes of our ancient connections, experience in whatever way we can, the richness of the treasure of the old ways, of our true heritage now hidden from us by the bars of our prisons, the burdens we carry that root us to the present and the chains of materialism. Which reminds me of a story….

The Coyote is laughing

The Coyote was a trickster character in folklore, he is cunning, devious, opportunistic and predatory – and his voice sounds like laughter. This story – which exists in various forms in many cultures tells us why we are as we are.

Once all people were wanderers moving with the seasons, following the animals that supplied their food, clothing and everything they needed to survive. To move was to live, to stop was to die. Then, the Coyote played a terrible trick on the people, he gave them the corn. The people thought it was a great and wonderful gift, but they did not see that those who accepted the gift of the corn had to stay in one place, they had to dig into the earth to plant it, spend their lives to tend it, bring water to it if the rain did not fall. They could not move south to warmer lands when the Winter came, they were forced to grow more corn so they had enough to sustain them through the time when the corn would not grow. And so, the people became slaves to the corn. No longer were they as free as the wild geese, the deer, or the buffalo. Other men then learned to steal from the slaves of the corn, and so there came the need to build strong walls that needed defending from attack and so there came always war between the people. So, not only did the Coyote's trick make men slaves it also made them the enemies of each other.

How much strife and death has resulted from this? Even today people go to war over resources – mostly oil in our time. The Second World War especially was concerned with the struggle to control the world's oil reserves and the struggle for oil still continues to this day. The history of the Middle East is one of wars about oil and it seems never to cease. The trick the Coyote played changed the course of humanity – although the question as to whether it was a wonderful gift or it made us slaves is irrelevant - because both outcomes are basically true. There is no doubt we have benefitted from our slavery in many ways but at such a terrible cost.

There was no really significant change to the way we lived because we were still tied to the land - until the advent of the Industrial Revolution beginning around 1750 when vast numbers of people began to leave their agricultural lives behind them to work in manufacturing industries in the crowded, unhealthy towns and cities. We might view the beneficial changes the Industrial Revolution brought about as another gift from the Coyote – for people were now enslaved to the mines, mills and factories, living in cities removing themselves even further away from their dependence on and connection with the land. The machines and the factories brought the slavery of the clock which separated day from night, men from women, parents from their children.

Fast forward to the 20th Century when a new technological revolution transformed humanity. This revolution was the most profound change in human history because it coincided with the development of computer technology, the contraceptive pill and the landings on the Moon. We gained for the first time a truly unique perspective of our world – we could see its image from another world and that has fundamentally changed our relationship with it.

We can see now that we are not the centre of the Universe, we are a fragile blue dot in the immensity of space, the only place where life exists as far as we know. Our very concept of reality has been transformed many times, from flat Earth to globe, from the sun orbiting the Earth to the Earth orbiting the sun, but now reality is being changed as never before and even the rational evidence of our own eyes is no longer enough to reassure us.

Artificial Intelligence may appear to work miracles, but it is still after all artificial. The Coyote has given us another wonderful gift and we are now more enslaved than ever.

As well as the perspective from another world and computer technology there was another unprecedented event that occurred in the 20th century – another gift from the Coyote – birth control. For the first time in human history women had the choice about becoming pregnant. This was of course a wonderful thing in countless ways, but those pills swallowed in their billions have polluted the environment leading to a steady decline in male fertility. Perhaps it was no coincidence that the role of the male began to be increasingly defined as dysfunctional and redundant, the rift between men and women torn open even wider. Populations are shrinking – at least certain sectors of the population. There have also been massive changes brought about by social engineering. Whole nations and their cultures are being eroded, mass migration is being encouraged and the roles of the very unit of human reproduction - a man and a woman have been redefined almost to the state of redundancy, the sanctity of marriage destroyed, the murder of the unborn normalised.

The human species is being redesigned and reprogrammed we are increasingly being forced to mate with machines rather than with each other - indeed most of our interactions are now performed by machines, actual human interaction is becoming ever more redundant and deemed inconvenient. Most people now communicate by their mobile phones, face to face real human contact is becoming rarer. Young men retreat from the world and play computer games instead of having real adventures. They are losing their role in the world by fighting digital battles and rescuing fantasy maidens. Men have essentially been left behind, discarded by the new order, their roles as hunters and providers increasingly obliterated and even though it is men who design, build and maintain just about everything that civilisation has become they are now culturally excluded, expendable lower cast drones now deemed less than human, secondary to the artificially created, hedonistic androgynous combined facsimile.

And what of young women? Women have been affected by the massive changes far more than men. Marxist-feminism has constructed a society where even though they have all the benefits and none of the responsibilities they are taught to believe they are victims who are oppressed by their fathers, brothers and sons. They have essentially been mated with the State for although they may still have the dubious right to give birth and raise children those children belong not to their mothers or fathers but to the State.

Many young women are obsessed with their own fantasy image. They live in a fantasy where they are assured they can have a rewarding career, always be stunningly attractive, have sex with as many people as they choose and ignore the realities of child rearing – which is what a woman's primary reason for being alive is. Biological sex is now being corrupted, children are being indoctrinated into perversions of what real existence is. This can only lead to our ultimate destruction as a species. We have been modified, neutered, incapacitated by those who rule us – we are like domesticated cattle, no longer free to wander, we are being de-sexed, de-educated, dumbed down and herded towards the slaughterhouse.

This inhumanity is being forced upon us under the age-old method of belief and fear – the same basic belief and fear mechanism that changed us from free wanderers into the slaves of the agricultural revolution. We are instructed by our rulers and the High Priests of our time that we must believe their propaganda otherwise the planet will freeze or boil, we must believe or we will be killed by starvation or pandemics caused by unseen viruses or swamped by overpopulation. These insanities that are being inflicted upon us now have been planned for many years but most people have not recognised the threats they have meekly obeyed, they've believed the lies rather than taken the trouble to look for themselves, they've traded their freedoms, their lives, their futures for the gifts the Coyote has given them. How the Coyote must be laughing?

All these changes are being forced upon us ignoring the thousands of years that shaped our beliefs, our emotions and our basic human psychology. We now inhabit a time governed by concepts and filled with technology that our predecessors would find incomprehensible, that they would regard as magic, yet for all the benefits of the technological miracles we are surrounded with we are physically little different from our ancestors and our hopes and fears, our perceptions of our world and each other are still affected by the vast amount of time we spent in the prehistoric 'Garden of Eden'.

And here I was on the Island in my alternative world, returned to a kind of Eden - learning – or more accurately relearning primaeval knowledge, reconnecting as much as is now possible with our distant predecessors, seeing at least some of what they could see, feeling at least some of what they felt, connecting with that far distant time when we were all connected with everything. Were the lessons I was learning applicable to others – perhaps to all of us?

> *The real problem of humanity is the following: We have Palaeolithic emotions, mediaeval institutions and*
> *God like technology.*

-    E. O. Wilson in Harvard Magazine 2009

From my new perspective I began to understand these changes, these stages of human existence. It's not evolution in the physical sense - it's more like revolutions that have been imposed on our minds, each one attempting to destroy the original template of what it is to be human. Yet that original template is still there beneath the colossal changes that have shaped our history. It's in our pre-history – in the thousands and thousands of generations of our collective unconscious (or perhaps more accurately sub-conscious) that the bedrock of humanity survives. I wonder if we can learn to access that bedrock, that ocean floor upon which we were all anchored and connected and in some way we might find our freedom from the tyranny that is now engulfing us?

The collective unconscious is common to all; it is the foundation of what the Ancients called the sympathy of things
-      C.G. Jung

I had been living on the island for a few years when I found another relevant connection to the distant past. Quite unknown to me at the time there was a few miles away from my Island a large area of high heathland behind a sizable village. This substantial hill must have been a large island in the inland sea and it surely must have been inhabited by ancient people. As it happens it was an area where archaeologists had found traces of Celtic people - a tribe known as the Iceni – which coincidentally were ruled by a warrior queen we know today as Boudica – the very name of my boat! Boudica revolted against the Roman conquerors of Britain, rampaging across England destroying every trace of them and their settlements. Her army destroyed Colchester then went on to burn the Roman city of London to the ground. The destruction was so utterly complete that there is a black, burnt layer of soil – known to archaeologists as the Boudica layer.

Boudica's luck ran out when the bulk of the Romans learned of her insurrection and their army returned from Wales where they had been engaged in fighting the Celtic Welsh. The Romans had cornered the Welsh on the Island of Anglesey where they had destroyed the Druid temples. Hurrying back along their superb road system they met up with Boudica's army and defeated them in a huge battle. Even though the Romans were outnumbered, their superior tactics carried the day – but the warrior queen was not taken alive – her body was spirited away from the battlefield. Nobody knows where she is buried or where the final battle took place, but when I walked the hill and let my senses roam free I somehow felt that this must have been one of her strongholds – perhaps she is buried there somewhere on the hill overlooking her realm.

There is no evidence to support my intuition, but the hill has always been known as Maid's Cross Hill and that clinches it for me. Also, now on the opposite side of the hill from the village there is a sprawling US base where jet fighter planes are stationed and nuclear weapons have been stored. Another echo connecting with a warlike past it seemed to me.

I can see that warfare really started when we ceased to be nomads and became farmers because our settlements had to be defended against those who would simply steal what had been produced. Villages built protective walls and the tools of hunting and farming became easily transformed into weapons. As the settlements grew into towns and cities the structure of societies changed and alongside those who actually produced the food there emerged the need for soldiers, smiths, carpenters, masons, craftsmen of all kinds and legions of administrators that had to be paid for.

Thus, the first economies grew in complexity each dependent on each other and all dependent on those who produced the food that sustained them all and all were governed by the priest classes and the powerful chieftains and rulers. All depended on the need for defence and the threat of war. Tribes grew into allied territories and then into nations. Unfortunately, it's warfare that has driven our economies, created the world we live in today and we can't change it for there is no practical alternative system available – unless we could somehow go back to being nomads – which seems impossible - we are stuck with it – or are we?

Now warfare is regarded as an instrument of national and social policy, the fact that a society is organised for any degree of readiness for war supersedes its political and economic structure, it defines the basic social system within which other social organisations must conspire with. This system has governed most human societies since they ceased to be nomadic and adopted agriculture. The permanent possibility of war is the foundation for stable government for it supplies the basis for general acceptance of political authority and it has ensured the subordination of the citizen to the state.

None are so hopelessly enslaved as those who falsely believe they are free

- Johann Von Goethe

If you've ever despaired that there always seems to be a war going on somewhere it's relevant to remind ourselves that not only does the world's economic systems thrive on it, everything we have in one way or another depends on the willingness of some people somewhere trying to wipe out some other people from somewhere else. It's become the way of things and however much we abhor the killing - the sacrifice of predominantly young men - we accept it as normal. It's not my idea of a good way to live but can there possibly be some other way to run the world?

Connection brings freedom from all those things that have no real value, no real purpose. Connection gives access to the flow of the Universe, the flow of life and the flow of the river is a gleaming silver metaphor of the force that bears me onward towards the universal ocean and I have no fear now of the clock ticking, or the journey, or the destination. Connection is when the world talks to you and you can listen. Connection is the voice of the Universe communicating, advising, recommending, guiding.

No wonder those who try to govern and manipulate us want the connection broken, no wonder they want us deaf and blind, confused, directionless, helpless. I think they are the present-day equivalent of the Neolithic priests who convinced us to give up our free wanderings to stay in one place and farm. Now in our time that ancient force to change us has come again, those who rule us are attempting to completely redefine us as human beings to change our identities and further destroy our connections with the Earth beneath our feet and the heavens above us.

Is it possible to learn from the distant past when we were closely attuned to the Universe, when we followed the natural rhythms and lived by natural laws? We can't forget what we have become, but there is the possibility that we might realise that by regaining at least some of what we've lost we might find a new direction – a way of freedom from the prison of our current incarnation, a different future – or is this hope just a dream of the past?

In the dreaming time we kept on moving, we followed the line
We kept going come rain or shine, we kept on moving through
the dreaming time
Walking with the wild ways we never numbered the passing of
the days
We measured our shadows in the sun and the wild ones
showed us when to return

Now we have cleared out the wildwood, torn the green flesh
from the earth

*Now we are rooted like the golden grain praying for the sun
to come back again*

We are planted here unwilling prisoners of our own fear

*Forced to fight against our own kind, we are sealed up in the
hive mind*

*We burn the bright flame in the frozen night, we dance around
it in the full moon's light*

*We keep the faith and the sickle keen spilling blood for the
white queen*

*But when we see the leaves fall and far horizons where the old
ways call*

*We long to follow where the wild herds wind to take us back
to the dreaming time*

The Dreaming Time – Poem by Les Richards

Connections

Sometimes I could really feel the pull, the river's strong voice whispered in my mind, 'come on, come on,' and it was almost painful to ignore it. This must be an echo of the migration urge that all nomads experienced and birds and animals still do. On a gorgeous Spring morning when the air was still and fragrant with all the new life and the water was almost motionless and there were sun sparkles and a fine mist, I knew it was going to be a beautiful day and what better way to spend it than on the river? If there was no one available to share it with me, or I had to go elsewhere on this perfect morning it was very frustrating – but if I was anticipating this and I had a companion then we prepared for an early departure – earlier the better because that's when the river was at its best. That was when the world was at its newest. Would you like to take a trip with me?

There was no need to pack a picnic because everything needed was right here – we were going travelling and home was going along with us. We simply disconnected the electric power cable, fired up the engine, cast off the mooring ropes and slid gently out of the marina, the boat glided past rows of other multi-coloured boats, my fellow Islanders waved a smiling farewell from their windows – they were staying while we were going, under the bridge, then we turned hard right avoiding the overhanging willows, then hard left on to the river and we were on our way. If you stood on the front deck, you could feel the change in your body, the subtle power of the river beneath you and you felt a release, a disconnection with everything you've left behind and you could sense you were connected now to the river and with that there was a wonderful peace – there were no problems, nothing mattered but the journey. This was why I lived this way - this was freedom. The engine chugged, the birds sang, the swans passed by and we were away, away from it all, off on the silver road.

The river ever onward flows and holds an open secret there within
Deep inside yet shining through the light that sparkles on its wrinkled skin
Today the images of tumbling clouds march beside the ripples as they race
Tonight, the fires of distant stars will shimmer in the mirror of its face

Poem - Les Richards

You got that wonderful feeling of leaving the outside world behind and engaging with the natural timeless world as the boat picked up just a little more speed and although we didn't build up to even walking pace for a while there is that realisation that you are the Captain, you are steering your own course, responsible for everything, paddling your own canoe so to speak. The long narrow form of the boat stretched out before you, the water parted before her bows, her smooth passage displaced the still water, the sun painted the reeds brilliant ochre, water diamonds sparkled. Astern, the river burbled from the prop and gently shimmered by her passing. The new green shoots of reeds and leaves were only just poking out but there was a green tinge to the willow branches so it would not be long. Spring was just beginning. There's no need to hurry, we simply watched the swans and geese, the heron lazily flapping as we passed by. We passed the washes – these are flood plains usually inhabited by flocks of Canada geese, but sometimes by cattle and a small herd of gorgeous horses running wild, the water was liquid mercury, sun spangled silk and we were gliding along the seam between two dimensions, reflected in each other.

Then there was the smell of everything. I'd never had a good sense of smell but I found that the longer I stayed out on the river the more sensitive my nose became. I imagine it was just that it was a sense I had forgotten to use or take much notice of. The boat itself exuded a heady cocktail of diesel oil and wood smoke mixed with the smell of the river which changed dramatically with the seasons and the weather. Every season has its smell, the dying off of vegetation in the Autumn, the fragrance of riverside flowers and plants in the Spring and Summer, the Winter too has its rich palette of smells. With the engine running there were exhaust fumes too, but 'Bou's engine ran much cleaner than many and so there was no following plume of dirty smoke, the shape of the hull seemed to disturb the water very little, the wake behind us was more like a bubbling Spring than a powerful thrust of agitated water.

Chuggin' along the silver road living a life that's free
We sing this song as we drift along the tiller man and me
Sixteen tons of British steel and a three pot Lister too
She's six feet wide and seventy long and everybody calls her
'Bou' Yes, everybody calls her 'Bou'

Up with the dawn in the misty morning up with the heron and
the kingfisher blue
There's not a thing I'd rather do than spend my time with you,
spend my time with you

Chuggin' along the silver road living a life that's free
We sing this song as we drift along the tiller man and me
The swans and the geese and the ducks on the river, the big
marsh harrier circling high
The winds in the willows sing along as we go drifting by, as
we go drifting by

Chuggin' along the silver road living a life that's free

We sing this song as we drift along the tiller man and me
At the end of the day there's a wild green mooring
Where the white owl flies when the sun goes down
Shimmering stars in the peaceful waters
Ripple in the reeds all around, ripple in the reeds all around
Chuggin' along the silver road living a life that's free
We sing this song as we drift along the tiller man and me

The Tiller Man and Me – Les Richards

I used to travel to some wild moorings on another tributary river. This place was for me the best portal to the Otherworld. The moorings were smack bang in the middle of a huge nature reserve that had been created to form as close as possible a Neolithic landscape. We would usually stay here for up to a week – it was the prime destination whatever time of year. There are fairly wide floodplains enclosed by earth banks and in the Summertime the grasses grow high. This section of the river is very old and it meanders a great deal, I believe it now runs in the opposite direction to what it used to originally. There has been extensive re-routing of the rivers and drainage channels over the centuries to drain the Fens but now the area is being progressively geo-engineered to return the landscape to its original state. There are extensive reed beds on one side of the river containing a multitude of species and it truly feels like you are in another country, a different world and it's a wonderful place for connecting to the past as well as the present. Here I really could experience the freedom of the nomad and the natural connection with the Universe such as the wild creatures we share the planet with still possess.

I do believe that somehow, someway we are constantly on the receiving end of some vast, universal consciousness. Although I was thankful for what I was receiving, it's fair to say that until I came to the Island I did not really appreciate or understand its full value or significance. My life has provided plenty of evidence for this. Think about it – at the one time in my life I needed to live in a monastery I actually was living in a monastery. I didn't have anything else though. In fact, I'd lost just about everything. You might say it was the 'Winter of my discontent' – but that would be putting it mildly. I won't tell you how I got myself into a place that was so grey and cold and dead – that's another story. Let's just say that life had put me in a situation that was not exactly one of life's sun-washed, verdant uplands, if you know what I mean.

Look, you can believe this or not, but I swear to you this story is true and it really happened to me. This was an event that caused me to ask myself just *what* exactly it was I did believe in. It also happened at the time I really needed that question to be asked on my behalf. It was in the bleak mid-Winter – as the Christmas Carol goes – but it wasn't Christmas – it was January or February time, when everything is grey and cold and dead, that time when the whole cycle of life is paused, the Earth at that degree of tilt that is as far as it goes and it hasn't really started to swing back yet. That's how things were for me, I was in a state where my life had tilted dramatically into a barren, desolation. I'd been in a place where I had first recognised and battled with the force we call evil. You may think evil does not really exist – I didn't, but I can assure you it does and when I was faced with it I was almost completely destroyed. I fought with evil and I did not win the battle, but having faced it I knew then it really did exist in the world. However, in the aftermath of my devastation the Universe provided me with exactly what I needed.

I must explain that I was not there as a monk. The monastery – which belonged to a Franciscan order, was completely empty apart from me. The place had been up for sale for a couple of years and there had been little interest in it. It was a bit of a shambles, you see, a large house built about the turn of the century with several incongruous additions built by the monks over the years. I was fortunate that the agents looking after the place allowed me to rent a tiny flat on the ground floor just so that someone would be around the place. It was a weird flat that had been made in the former reception area of the monastery. The front door was wide and there were glazed panels either side and from the outside it might have looked as if it still was the main entrance - except the short drive from the main road was covered with dead leaves and the rusty main gate was padlocked shut.

It was a Saturday afternoon, about that time when everyone who is going somewhere has already gone, but has not yet returned and it was grey and cold and dead outside, the road beyond the boundary trees was quiet and empty and so I was not expecting a visitor.

There was a knock on the front door. I went and opened it. A strange man about thirty-ish stood there. He was well wrapped up against the cold and he had a bicycle – but not like any bicycle I'd ever seen. This bike was laden with planks of wood tied along the frame and on the carrier a large wooden box. There were tools tied all over the thing too – saws, planes, chisels, hammers. I wondered how on Earth anyone could actually ride a bike loaded up like that. The guy looked weird too. He looked like a bit of a hippy, but as I said he was well wrapped up against the cold. He had a scarf wrapped around his lower face, but he had a beard and his eyes were blue and strange – like he was kind of disconnected from the cold and the magnitude of the journey ahead.

I imagine he thought I was one of the monks as he asked me whether there were any jobs he could do around the place. He said he was a carpenter. I explained that I was certainly no monk and that apart from me the place was empty. He didn't seem at all put out. Then my curiosity caused me to ask where he'd come from. He told me he'd come from 'up north' and was making his way to London. He didn't have a northern accent though. We chatted for a few minutes and then he made to leave. I looked at his bike and wished him a safe journey. He turned and smiled back at me as he wobbled off down the empty road. It was a knowing smile that I found somehow comforting.

"You know Jesus was a carpenter," he called out. It made me think. What if it was Him? I'd never even offered him a coffee. Now you could say this was all pure coincidence and my visitor was just a wandering nutter – but why him, why there, why then?

It took a little time for things to resolve, but I can remember very well how it happened. I was out in a nearby field of wild grasses and flowers and as usual my mind was going crazy trying to think of a way out of my situation. Then for some reason – maybe it was something to do with my natural surroundings - I let go of trying to solve my problems. I said to the Universe 'I can't sort this out, I've tried everything I know and nothing works – in fact everything I try only makes things worse. Well. I'm going to stop trying, I'm letting it all go. Now it's up to you - the Universe to sort out – I'm trusting you to do what you will with me and I will accept your will'. I was immediately overcome with relief, my problems were no longer in my hands – and do you know what? Within a few weeks everything in my life changed, my problems went away and my life took a miraculous new direction.

It seemed like I had been given another miracle. In Taoism there is a concept called *Wu Wei*. It means to take action by taking no action – in other words to let go and let the universe take action and to trust that the equilibrium will naturally be restored. For me it was. My life took off in another direction but the Universe had a great deal more to teach me, I still had a great deal to learn.

I know the way of all things by what is within me

- Lao Tzu

There has been one connection I discovered in my life that I could have done without, but I suppose it was part of my journey to be given the knowledge of its existence and so I include it here as a warning - not everything we can connect with from the Universe is benign.

The word 'evil' is bandied about a great deal but thank God people don't have the opportunity to really meet the horrific reality of the force of evil. It seems a word plucked from the Middle Ages, from the excesses of religious fanaticism, but evil – that is the force of evil certainly exists in our own time. People watch horror movies, they seem fascinated by gruesome stories, they delight in absorbing tales of terrible murders, rapes, cannibalism, brutal inhuman crimes and feed on every forensic detail. Women in particular are attracted to this kind of 'entertainment' – which is strange as they are more often than not the primary victims of such barbarity. I can assure you, if anyone comes face to face with the reality of evil then they would not immerse themselves in these themes. It would be the last thing they would do.

Children are infected by the theme of horror. The celebration of Halloween has become a multi-million cash cow. Like many negative gifts that have come from the United States of America Halloween has been firmly grafted into English 'culture'. As a festival having its roots in ancient paganism it was almost extinct when I was growing up but now it is exploited to the maximum particularly to children.

I was staying at a friend's house once and I woke up to find there was a corpse wrapped in black plastic bin liners hanging from a tree outside the house next door. My friend informed me that the people next door had done it to celebrate Halloween with their young children. It wasn't a real body of course, but it looked just like one. Why would any parent subject their children to something like that as 'fun'? Could those parents imagine that hanging corpse being real? Evil has come into the everyday world in the form of a festival for young children, and the gullible people who indulge it surely have no concept of what real evil is.

I have seen evil in relatively few people in my life and each time I was shocked and devastated. Once I saw it in a child who had witnessed its mother's murder, I've seen evil within adults too. It can live within those who have been terribly abused, it can hide behind what seems innocent, it can be beguiling and entice the unwary. Evil is a force in the Universe that can inhabit human beings and when you come across it in an individual you will be devastated by it. Evil can be transmitted from one person to another by an evil act upon that person and then that unfortunate person too will carry the evil force within them. Evil infects whoever it touches - that is how it thrives in the world, evil is a parasitic predator that preys on the souls of human beings – especially the vulnerable, the young and the naïve. If you should sense it in anyone you should avoid them at all costs. Don't ever think you can fight it or cure it – you cannot - and to deny its existence is to put yourself in peril.

I believe that unarmed truth and unconditional love will have the final word in reality.
This is why right, temporarily defeated, is stronger than evil triumphant

Martin Luther King Jr.

Do we have souls? Surely, we are not merely bodies of flesh and bone. We surely have a life spirit that shines within us and when we die that spirit leaves us. That belief in the soul is very common throughout the world's religions and has existed in human thought throughout our history. Some people believe that they have memories of past lives, former incarnations and there are reliably documented instances of this. Some religions teach that we have many incarnations, thousands upon thousands and that we return to a new life to learn that which we failed to learn in the previous one. This belief gives rise to the concept of karma – which suggests that our actions in our current lives and our previous lives decide our fates in future incarnations.

You can see it's an effective belief in that it helps guide our behaviour and can make us consider the consequences of our actions. Belief in the existence of the soul might be to some people wishful thinking, a placebo that deceives us into accepting the insignificance of our human existence, but it must be a fearful thing to believe that our lives serve no Universal purpose, that when we die we are nothing but oblivion. From all I've seen, experienced and researched I believe that we do have souls and that the purpose of our lives is to learn, to become ever closer to God the Universal Spirit and when we die we leave our bodies behind us and our essence becomes one with the Universe. Maybe we are born again and have new lives to continue to learn, to grow ever closer to the perfection God requires of us. We can choose what to believe of course, but I believe it's better to live without fear of life or death.

There was one connection I did not discover – the connection I'd always had. When you are a child you know nothing but your own consciousness, everyone else's is isolated so we can't know what anyone else is thinking or what reality is for them. We only inhabit our own minds and that can be a lonely place. Growing up was always lonely for me – I couldn't really connect with others my age or come to that anyone else. I was isolated in a loveless wilderness yet I had the spiritual connection that I somehow knew to be real although no one else around me seemed to share it. It was in that connection that I knew the existence of the power of love. It never left me in spite of the trials of my life although I can only believe it came from the Universe and was within me.

You can call this God's Love if you choose to. I wouldn't argue with that definition. The spirit of the Universe is God and it is the power of Love. We live in a world where Love and Evil fight to control both it and us. It is incumbent on us therefore to seek that Universal Spirit and connect with it in our lives – only then we are fully whole, only then can that Spirit inhabit us.

The Tao that can be told is not the eternal Tao
The name that can be named is not the eternal name.
The Tao is both named and nameless
As nameless it is the origin of all things.
Ever desireless, one can see the mystery;
Ever desiring, one sees only the manifestations.
And the mystery itself is the doorway to all understanding.

1st Verse of the Tao Te Ching - Lao-tzu

I sometimes talk to people who have found spiritual conversions in their lives, the discovery of knowing God, or Jesus or both. As adults they claim to be born again, they sometimes get baptised and find revelation by joining various churches. Christianity as a religion seems a labyrinth of often conflicting beliefs, dogmas and sometimes strict parameters. Originally it was the Roman Catholic Church that defined the religion. The Church of England which I knew of when I went to school has disappeared now and has fractured into a plethora of guises; Protestants, Restorational, Pentecostal, Gospel, Revivalist, Methodists, Baptists Charismatics'…each with their own definitions of what God is. Some appear to me as downright dysfunctional – people rant, speak in tongues, evangelise their own personal interpretations. It all seems far removed from the simple teachings of Jesus. It all seems far removed from my own understanding of God – which is to me the Universal Spirit. In that respect Taoism - which isn't a religion and simply defines itself as 'The Way' - speaks the closest to the truth to me.

Vast indeed is the ultimate Tao, spontaneously itself, apparently without acting,
End of all ages, existing before Earth and existing before heaven,
Silently embracing the whole of time, continuing uninterrupted through all eons,
In the East it taught father Confucious, in the East it converted the Buddha,
Taken as a pattern by a hundred kings, transmitted by generations of sages,
It is the ancestor of all doctrines, the mystery beyond all mysteries.

-    A Ming Rock Inscription 1556

Then there is love – we must talk of love. I've thought about love a great deal – I think we all have. It's just a small word yet we use it to describe a whole range of feelings and emotions just that one four letter word. You know, the Eskimos have at least 52 different words for snow - so why is it we only have one word for love? Why is it we seem reluctant to define the different kinds of love – it seems to be almost a taboo subject.

What exactly is love? There is the love a parent has for their children and there is of course the love between human beings – friends, family members and there is a wider all-embracing love that some people feel for the sick, the disabled – those who perhaps need it the most and indeed for all humanity. Their love is especially needed in this world. It's hard to imagine that this compassion and caring aspect of love was not always with us and that for much of history the sick and injured were merely left to die. Life then was far from sacred and callous brutality was regarded as normal. That we now try to preserve life, heal the sick and injured and attempt to ease the lives of those who are burdened with disabilities is arguably the greatest triumph of love in action in the world.

There is the hunger for ordinary bread, and there is the hunger for love, for kindness, for thoughtfulness and this is the great poverty that makes people suffer so much

-    Mother Teresa of Calcutta

This quote reminds me of an interesting story. I once had a kind but rather naïve friend who was very wealthy and he told me of the experience he'd had with Nobel Prize winning Catholic Nun Mother Teresa in Calcutta. He had gone to India to visit his old school friend who was a wealthy Maharaja and aware that she was becoming something of a legend with her work with the poor, sick and dying people he decided to visit her, make a donation and collect a personal anecdote or two he might use to impress some of his somewhat shallow acquaintances at dinner parties.

He arrived at the Missionaries of Charity and was met by one of the nurses who told him that Mother Teresa was busy working and couldn't spend time socialising. He was a little irritated but he wasn't going to leave without meeting this woman who was regarded as a living Saint and so he told the nurse that if he could meet her for a few minutes, he would make a sizable donation. The nurse went off to enquire and a few minutes later the famous Mother Teresa appeared – a tiny shrivelled figure wrapped in a worn Sari and wearing the familiar 'tea towel' headdress. She shook his hand and thanked him for the donation but she admonished him politely and suggested to him that there were plenty of poor, desperate people in his own country that might benefit from his attention. Now that is wisdom and love in action.

It is perhaps an interesting comparison when you consider that Diana Princess of Wales died on the 31st of August 1997 – at the time of her death she had a net worth of £21,000,000. Mother Teresa died on the 5th September 1997 – just five days later - she owned just two saris and a bucket. Who is the most remembered and who showed the most love and compassion in this world? It's an interesting question.

Hello, is it me you're looking for?

-       Lionel Ritchie

There is the love that preoccupies us most of all, the love that attracts people to each other – the love that is celebrated in art, poetry, literature and popular culture. Is this really love though, or is it a refined version of lust - for after all, its purpose does seem ultimately to be to bring about procreation? However we may define it, this love is the emotion that brings us so much joy, ecstasy, grief and pain in our lives. We seem to pursue it blindly, searching every face for the one face that will herald the arrival of the person we believe we are destined to couple with. This quest fills every aspect of our lives, the books we read, the movies we watch, the things we buy, the things we do are all underpinned by this crazy search.

We pursue this dream with the zeal of a salmon swimming up river driven by the primaeval urge to mate, but we humans don't just content ourselves with fertilising eggs, we have to pursue and possess the object of our lusts. We behave like animals, males fighting for supremacy to mate with the most suitable females.

At least in nature the animals seemed to have worked it out but we humans seem unable to get together without a great deal of pain, grief and confusion and even when we find a mate staying together is often harder than meeting in the first place.

You who never arrived in my arms. Beloved who were lost from the start
I don't even know what songs would please you.
I have given up trying to recognize you in the surging wave of the next moment.
All the immense images in me - the far off deeply felt landscape, cities, towers and bridges and unsuspected turns in the path
And those powerful lands that were once pulsing with the life of the gods –
All rise within me to mean You who forever elude me.

You beloved, who are all the gardens I have ever gazed at, longing.
An open window in a country house – and you almost stepped out, pensive to meet me.
Streets that I chanced upon you had just walked down them and vanished.
And sometimes, in a shop, the mirrors were still dizzy with your presence and,
Startled, gave back my too sudden image.
Who knows? Perhaps the same bird echoed through both of us
Yesterday, separate, in the evening...

-       Rainer Maria Rilke 1875-1926 Austrian Poet.

Some people believe that romantic love was invented by travelling troubadours in the French courts of the 12th-13th Century, that it is a cultural construction, a distraction from the usual practical unions of people marrying for power and wealth or even to keep the peace between nations. Undoubtedly there are today cultures in which people marry for practical reasons – as in Indian societies where even today it is common for the bride and groom to be chosen by professional matchmakers who select couples based on their financial and social compatibility. Unsurprisingly these arranged marriages can be more successful than those that are based on romantic attraction, for they tend to avoid the financial stresses that western marriages can face. That is not to say that the individuals in these arrangements are immune from sexual liaisons beyond marriage.

Let not to the marriage of true minds admit impediments
Love is not love which alters when it alteration finds
Or bends with the remover to remove
O, no it is an ever fixed mark that looks on tempests and is
never shaken
It is the star to every wandering bark whose worth's unknown
Although his height be taken.
Love's not times fool, though rosy lips and cheeks within his
bending compass come
Love alters not with his brief hours and weeks
But bears it out even to the edge of doom
If this be error and upon me proved I never writ, nor no man
ever loved

-       Sonnet CXV1 William Shakespeare

At a traditional Christian wedding the bride and groom vow to stay together always - no matter what comes – which is necessary for raising stable children and building a stable society, but life in the modern world has increasingly eroded the religious glue that held people together. The reality of people's lives today makes the expectation to remain together for life an increasingly rare aspiration. With the best will in the world the truth is that not everyone can achieve the ideal and how could they be expected to when their marriage becomes abusive or one partner in the arrangement fails to keep the contract. Why should someone stay in a loveless marriage when they might find fulfilment elsewhere? People fall in and out of love – however it's defined. Everyone is bound to deal with these situations as best they can. All is fair in love and war they say. Nothing is forever, everything has its season, everything is born and dies – that is the way of things. We can't hold on to anything or anyone – eventually we have to let go. If we are fortunate in finding somebody to share the journey we are blessed, but they must walk freely beside us on their own path.

Personally, I've always found it easy to love and to apply love in whatever I do in my life but like everyone else I've been hurt by love and I've been guilty of neglecting to love. I've found it hard to forgive sometimes and I've blanked people from my life rather than deal with problems in another way. Betrayal is a hard pill to swallow for me but I know I have betrayed others in my time. I don't expect to be forgiven – if I am then I'm grateful that those people can do that - but for me I would rather leave my errors and my failings behind on the path to die and hope that I've learned to do better in future. Love is something we all need for sure - but is love for receiving - or is it for giving?

One of the saddest things is to see love falter and die, but it is only at the second level that this happens.
At the third level love never falters, it has an integral strength.
At the fourth level it develops an unquenchable radiance.
At the fifth level, if you are so fortunate, you are part of the universal radiance

The Way and the Wilderness – Kenneth Robinson

It is clear to me that love is a powerful force in the world and that it is responsible for how we live our lives in countless ways. When we look for love are we merely seeking to find the love our parents showed us when we were born and as infants are we pursuing something beyond that? As love is an independent force in the world, can it find us, infect us, turn our lives upside down quite unexpectedly, can it drive us to act irrationally, to do things that make no logical sense, to become helpless prisoners of its overwhelming influence on our lives? Can love even kill us or cause us to end our own lives or those of others? Certainly, it can. Love is so powerful, so complex and multi-faceted that perhaps it defies categorisation, perhaps we use only the one word 'love' because to attempt any kind of classification is impossible. For me, the following words come close…

Love possesses not nor would it be possessed; for love is sufficient unto love. When you love you should not say 'God is in my heart', but rather, 'I am in the heart of God,'

And think not that you can direct the course of love, for love, if it finds you worthy, directs your course. Love has no other desire but to fulfil itself.

But if you love and must needs have desires let these be your desires: To melt and be like a running brook that sings its melody to the night;

To know the pain of too much tenderness;

To be wounded by your own understanding of love;

And to bleed willingly and joyfully;

To wake at dawn with a winged heart and give thanks for another day of loving;

To rest at the noon hour and meditate love's ecstasy;

To return home at eventide with gratitude;

And then to sleep with a prayer for the beloved in your heart and a song of praise upon your lips.

Extract from 'The Prophet' – Kahlil Gibran

I read somewhere that the people who are the hardest to love are those who need loving the hardest. Jesus spent his time on Earth with tax collectors, prostitutes, lepers, adulterers, the sick, the downtrodden, the criminals, the people who were the 'hardest to love' – and even when he was close to death, He asked God to forgive those who crucified Him. Clearly, he knew what love was and He tried to teach us by his own example. It's hard to love those who are the hardest to love but they are the ones who have the greatest need - that was His teaching. Can love always overcome though?

Our world is in a dire situation right now, it seems that it is descending into complete madness, never has evil been so powerful and strong and we all see the affect around us – horrific wars, family breakdown, massive addiction, crushing poverty, rampant crime, the corruption of our children, useless politicians who seem hell bent on destroying everything that is logical and good. What can we do against this tide of despair? Surely, we need the kind of love Jesus spoke of, we need Him to help us to learn how to love, to love each other and especially those who need loving the hardest.

Nietzsche the German philosopher stated in the 1880's that 'God was dead' because most intelligent people no longer believed in the existence of a supreme being or heaven and hell therefore, they had no fear of judgement, no fear of the ultimate consequences of their actions. The spiritual glue that had bound people together, tempered their behaviour, provided them with morality and structured human society was weakening, causing the breakdown of a belief system that had served since the beginning of the Christian era. Nietzsche prophesied that in the next century this lack of belief would lead to great wars fought between what he called 'barbaric brotherhoods' and that humanity would struggle through the remainder of the 20th century and the early part of the 21st century on the remaining echoes of the God based religion until there would come a time of the 'total eclipse of all values'. It seems obvious to me that Nietzsche's prophecy was accurate for we are now at that point in our history and in the vacuum caused by the absence of God pure evil has come to govern the world.

The individual is handicapped by coming face to face with a conspiracy so monstrous he cannot believe it exists

    – J. Edgar Hoover, 1956, speaking of Communism

Tyranarchy

One Summer's Day I was chugging down the river with a friend when we witnessed a Fenland Blow. A Blow happens when the soil becomes very dry – which is not that often it must be said. The soil is very rich and black in colour due to the fact that this whole area was an inland sea not so very long ago. It grows wonderful green vegetables but when it gets dry and the west wind blows it can lift the soil into the sky. It's quite an apocalyptic spectacle actually and it reminded me of images of the dust bowl in 1920's America. That's what happens if you mess with nature I suppose. It's scary to witness the very soil blowing away in dark brown clouds. It's scary and unnatural. It's apocalyptic.

We couldn't know it then, but an apocalypse was coming to us all in a few years and it wouldn't be a semi-natural event like the soil blowing away in one part of our Waterworld. What was coming would blow everything away, everything that people had known as normal, as the ground beneath our feet, our whole perception of the world we live in and how it works, everything would change – and not for the better.

It wasn't as though I had not seen it coming – I had, but it was the form it would take that was the surprise. I had been forewarned by things that had happened to me in the 1980's. As a result of the traumatic events which had happened in my own life I was forced to ask questions. Caused me to re-reassess everything that was going on in the world around me. It was a personal apocalypse and the ground beneath my feet was blown away like I'd never imagined.

Throughout history there was always some megalomaniac who wanted to rule the world; the Greeks with Alexander the

Great, the Romans, the Holy Roman Empire, then various European Empires had a shot at it. In the 20th Century as Nietzsche predicted Marx, Lenin, Hitler also tried it.

Those who plot to rule the world are not like the fictional villains who sit around scheming while they stroke white cats. The real tyrants are those who conquer by manipulating money. Money buys resources to be traded, oil and pharmaceuticals mainly, it starts wars, changes governments, exterminates whole races if they're inconvenient to their plans.

Money is their global weapon and ordinary people mostly cannot understand how or why these psychopaths do what they do. An empire is not enough these days, a collection of nations is hardly worth bothering over – these days they want the whole world and they'll tell the peasants anything to get their way – the Earth is freezing, the Earth is boiling, the Ozone layer is disappearing, the ice caps are melting, their strategies are built on the fear and the hopes of helpless people – much like those of the Neolithic priests I imagine.

When you look into the abyss the abyss looks back

-      Nietche

The digital concentration camp is being constructed around us and unlike the 1930's when Hitler rose to power there is no free country we can run for to escape its high fences. With world-wide total surveillance there will arise what amounts to an omnipresent global police force that will punish every infraction, every free thought and action that is not in the global rule book. There can be no free elections, no democracy, no individuality.

This is not science fiction, it is happening now. The world state they are building uses eco-religion – fears of massive environmental catastrophe to herd the masses towards the prison gates. They've created numerous enemies to be hated and feared, created wars, famines, even scared us with threats of asteroid impacts, super volcanoes, melting ice caps and alien incursions. They have isolated us, divided us and even attempted to make us hate ourselves. All the multi-faceted tools of modern media are employed to divide and conquer us, manipulate our thoughts and perceptions, prevent us from living freely, loving and procreating naturally.

Practically every movie is about wars or environmental catastrophes, rogue viruses, zombie apocalypses. We are undergoing a comprehensively implemented, sophisticated form of physical, emotional and psychological slavery. The system of war-based economy has controlled dangerous anti-social tendencies, thwarted any serious rebellion and coerced compliance and social allegiance.

Now, we are constantly subjected to a deliberately crafted narrative of how the world should be and how we should think and live. This dogma is thrown at us constantly by our governments by a compliant and strictly controlled mainstream media. We are not trusted to have our own individual opinions or feelings anymore. The State knows best.

In my lifetime things have totally reversed. Communism was always regarded as the enemy of Capitalism and Democracy. Millions of people died in wars and revolutions trying to keep the world free from dictatorships, but somewhere along the way free markets, free speech and national borders of the 'free world' have been deemed obsolete. The creation of a World State in the image of the former Communist power blocks is well underway.

*Communism is not [and never was] a creation of the masses
to overthrow the Banking establishment, but rather a creation of
the Banking establishment to overthrow and enslave the people.*

- Anthony J. Hilder

Evil is so malignant, so unbelievably powerful that it remains
incomprehensible to many people, yet the global plan for what
we and our world is to become has been freely available for
decades. Few of us bothered to look at the plan but we should
have taken the time to do so. Instead, most people, the vast
majority continued to enjoy the 'gifts of the coyote' instead of
searching the horizon for what was coming for us.

*The ideal tyranny is that which is ignorantly self-administered
by its victims.*
*The most perfect slaves are, therefore, those which blissfully
and unawaredly enslave themselves.*

- Dresden James

Now the terrible truth is beginning to hit home, increasingly
people are awakening to the horror that is the future. This plan is
far more than the by-pass or the housing development that our
local authorities have lurking in the labyrinths of their planning
departments. This plan is not going to be an annoying
inconvenience, this plan is already forcing millions of people on
vast migrations, cramming them into cities in Europe and north
America. The cities we're being herded into will get bigger, taller
and increasingly more violent, they are already being digitally
controlled, ring fenced by unseen walls from which escape will
be impossible.

It is a new religion that underwrites this madness, a religion
like all religions constructed with the two universal myths of

belief and fear – the same myths that ended our free wanderings of the pre-agricultural era. Then it was the fear of the Winter of death that could only be placated by human sacrifice to ensure the return of the Spring, next came the religion of the Christ who took on the sacrifice, that threatened the fires of hell for those who didn't conform and promised a life after death for those who did conform. Now we are being coerced into believing that the Earth will be destroyed by rogue climate catastrophes which we humans are responsible for. And so, our unelected masters tell us there must be a colossal human sacrifice to the environmental goddess Gaia, there are far too many of us and we are a cancer on the planet.

In the event that I am reincarnated I would like to return as a deadly virus to contribute something to solving overpopulation.

-      H.R.H. Prince Philip husband of Queen Elizabeth 2nd.

When the pandemic hit us, I was surprised that so many of the Islanders believed every word of the propaganda and marched forward to receive the 'safe and effective' vaccine. There were some – including myself who didn't go along with it. Fortunately, living on the Island it was easier to resist – but it was a strange and terrifying time in which everything changed.

There is a crime taking place so enormous that many of us do not yet grasp the magnitude of it. There has never been such a crime perpetrated in human history. When we think of genocide, we automatically think of Nazi Germany's Holocaust, Mao in the Chinese Cultural Revolution, Stalin in the Soviet Union, perhaps Rwanda, maybe the Cambodian killing fields genocide has been committed many times – but this crime – this crime, that is happening now - is far in excess of genocide. Understandably it is only just being assimilated by our collective consciousness.

Indeed, this crime is so far beyond comprehension that we need a new word to describe it. Humanicide – the extermination of a particular people or race is not sufficiently descriptive of what is happening now. This time the aim is to exterminate a vast proportion of the whole world's population.

This is the greatest war in the history of humanity – a war that has run in parallel with the countless international conflicts. It isn't nation against nation, or even religion against religion, for now the world's economy is controlled by a powerful elite who have taken it upon themselves to impose their own vision of how the world must be. The world they are building through the imposition of mass media propaganda, pseudo-religion, corrupt education systems and perverted social engineering will mean the destruction of billions of human beings. Only a miracle it seems can save us.

Of all tyrannies a tyranny sincerely exercised for the good of its victims may be the most oppressive.
-       C.S. Lewis

Miracles can happen – I can testify to that. Surely the world needs a miracle now. We seem to be helpless in the face of such overwhelming power stacked against us, the forces of evil seem to have the upper hand - but the situation is so volatile anything may happen – one single incident could change everything – like a butterfly's wings fluttering may lead to a typhoon in the Pacific Ocean – or a President may move his head a fraction and an assassin's bullet graze his ear.

In my time I never expected the Berlin Wall to come down or the Soviet Union to crumble. I never expected the Cuban missile crisis and it seems a miracle that the world wasn't nuked to oblivion. Growing up devouring all the promises of a shining new future I'd expected that by now there would be bases on the

Moon and Mars, that cancer would be cured and that poverty would be eliminated – and it seems perverse to me that so many miracles *haven't* happened, but only God dispenses miracles and only God knows how things will pan out. We can only pray and believe that the Universal Spirit will triumph.

Sometimes, people tell you things – examples of their own personal miracles - like the old man I talked with when I was in my early thirties. He'd been in the Merchant Navy in WW2 and his ship had been torpedoed in the middle of the Atlantic Ocean. The ship sank and he and a few of his mates were left floating alone in their life jackets. They had been at sea long enough to know that the chances of rescue were negligible and so they thought they were dead men. Then a miracle happened. A Royal Navy destroyer appeared and the men cheered in relief thinking they were going to be rescued – but just as they were about to hauled from the water the destroyer picked up a U-boat on its Asdic underwater locator and the Captain had to choose whether to rescue the half dozen men or go and hunt the German submarine which could sink many more ships and lose their vital cargoes and perhaps hundreds of men. Of course, there was no choice, the Captain's responsibility was to go and hunt the U-boat. The survivors in the water were crushed, their miracle rescue was a cruel twist of fate and they all knew they were certain to die now for they understood that the Destroyer might chase the U-boat for days and the chances of being found again were zero. However, after an hour or so the destroyer lost contact with the U-boat and returned to rescue the men in the water. That was surely a miracle.

We can believe in miracles, believe in the power of good, of love to rescue us. I've known miracles, more than my share I thought, but there was one more coming my way – the biggest and best ever – and therein lies my personal faith and hope. My time on the Island was coming to an end though I didn't expect it. Things had changed in the Waterworld, the toxic outer world had gradually invaded, there had been more and more people, more escapees, more boats and the innocence had been eroded, the connections harder and harder to make, the wildness was fading and it was clear that it was time to leave. Was I unhappy about this? Not really for I'd had my time on the Island when it was at its best and it had given me so much, the Universe had given me this place to learn from, to heal in, to be restored and now it had given me the one thing I still needed – that one person I was destined to share a new journey with. It was quite unexpected when I met her – but that is how miracles are. Some people meet that special person who makes them both whole when they are young. I know a couple who have been together for 70 years – that's a whole lifetime. Some people never find the other half of their soul. That's a tragedy.

The miracle is not to fly in the air, or walk on the water but to walk on the earth

-       Chinese proverb

Then there was the time I was doing some voluntary work for a Charity. On Saturdays I used to pick up the things from people who had donated to the Charity shop. Often this would involve collecting the possessions – usually clothes - of an elderly parent who had died. As you might imagine, these were very emotional occasions and I would spend a little time talking with the relative of the deceased - usually the daughter – it seemed to be the least I could do, after all they were handing over personal things to go to somebody else who they wouldn't know at all. It seemed to me there ought to be something said, something passed on of that deceased person. So, if they wanted to – and they almost always did – they talked and I listened. It was always an honour to share these conversations.

One day I went to this old Lady's bungalow to pick up some items she wanted rid of. She was very friendly and asked me if I wanted a cup of tea. We sat in her small living room talking about this and that. She told me that she'd recently had some things stolen, the thieves had taken some pieces of old furniture. She admitted that she never locked her door so it wasn't surprising, but she didn't seem to be angry about it. Then I noticed there was an old black and white framed photograph on the mantelpiece and I asked who it was. With a loving smile she took down the picture and told me that it was her husband who had been killed in the First World War. They hadn't been married for very long at all she said, but she'd never married again or sought the love of any other man – she told me he was the man for her and there could be no other. There is such treasure when you take the time to connect with people, they have so much to teach us.

I once came across an old book about Alchemy. I'd always thought that Alchemy was some cranky practice carried out by mediaeval philosophers attempting to understand science or most of the time trying to turn ordinary metal into gold – but I had obviously been misinformed. According to the book this was not the case at all. The whole thing about turning base metal into gold was actually an analogy that represented turning matter into spirit. As you might imagine the established church was not happy about the Alchemists and their philosophies. After all, the Christian Church was and still is the Establishment and since the Council of Nicene in AD 325 it's controlled the western world – that is until the 1960's when the Global Establishment dreamed up the various versions of 'Climate Crisis' as a new substitute religion to replace the decline in the old one. It's basically the same belief and fear, heaven and hell and of course there are its prophets and heretics just the same.

The Alchemists and their knowledge were excluded from the world and rigorously censored and ridiculed. But with the perspective that I'd gained from living in my wilderness I could begin to understand where the Alchemists were coming from. It seems they were the custodians of a great deal of ancient wisdom - wisdom that became increasingly unattainable to the people and here I was learning to connect with the Universal spirit and learning that most of the real 'gold' has been denied to us by the way we have been forced to live. The Alchemists had a formula to explain it. It goes like this; man =2 woman =3 which adds up to five. Five is the number that represents what they called the Quintessence – the perfect harmony. So now we have 3+2=5 but they added another number -1 which represented the Divine, God the Universal Spirit.

Love is composed of a single soul inhabiting two bodies.

- Aristotle

The formula is so simple when you really think about it – 3+2=5=1. It should be explained to every child, every man and woman but alas, our masters do not want us to know the secret formula of life, the universe and everything. If everyone understood this truth then what a world it could be? The basic unit of humanity is *binary* – it's not one man or woman it is one man *and* one woman. From this pair comes the family, the clan, the tribe and the nation. Nations are composed of peoples and cultures that are diverse. Those that control us are attempting to build a One World State in which these differences are ignored. Therefore, they have attempted to destroy the basic unit; to keep us divided, they've destroyed the building block of humanity by every means they can employ. Why is this not being taught to the young? It seems to me the most profound and vital information we need to understand. And that is why it is not being taught, why this simple equation is almost unheard of, unknown, that is why this formula, this vital truth has been hidden throughout history of civilization, but now you know it.

Solutions?

Already there is a growing movement of people seeking self-sufficiency, who are trying to live beyond the digital walls that are being constructed to imprison us all. These people grow their own food, raise a few animals, where possible build their own homes and use alternative energy, they trade and barter, home educate their children and avoid the old-world ways that have brought us to this pivotal moment. They may seem like farmers, but if they are to survive and prosper they must not repeat the same mistakes the first people who became rooted to the land made. There must be no more religion that demands sacrifice, no more priests that tell us what to believe, no more legions of administrators and if it be possible no more soldiers. A new way must not have an economy as it exists at the moment. It seems to me that there has to be a massive change in our perceptions of what we really are. The economies of the world are now even more based on warfare than when we ceased to be nomadic. If we could somehow break the long-established war + sacrifice = economy trinity that drives the world what a future there could be. Perhaps a future that unites us instead of dividing us?

Marxism has spawned racism, feminism, homosexual evangelism and transgenderism as social mechanisms to isolate and create a homogenised version of the human species, domesticated and easy to control. This nightmare vision of life in the World State, is portrayed as a shining future devoid of war and hunger where everyone is deemed 'equal' – a marvellous 'gift' that we must accept to ensure our survival as well as that of the planet. This 'gift' however is another trick the Coyote has played upon us. Warfare runs the world's economies more than ever before, it is not just promoted between nations or races. Now the binary unit that creates human life has been turned to declare war upon itself. You have to admit it's one global hell of an achievement.

When people believe in absurdities, they commit atrocities

\-   Voltaire

Why can't the psychopaths of the unelected globalist organisations, the monstrous architects of our destruction leave us be? I don't think they can allow it. I don't think there are any nomads left on the planet now – but there might be somewhere. Even in the remotest places everyone has a mobile phone. Before long, if our masters have their way it won't be an object we carry, it will be biologically included within us - another un-human organ as indispensable as a kidney or a liver.

Can we ever become nomads again? No, not in the original way, but we can travel in our minds, we can recapture what has been stolen from us and surely, we deserve to have our property back. The good news is we won't have to follow an animal herd, or leave the old and sick in the dust of our passing. We can move across the inner landscape of our minds where the journey and the destination still exists. There we may find again the freedom we once had and recapture the forgotten wisdoms that we once naturally inherited. When we are united again with the gifts from our time of innocence in the primaeval Garden of Eden, then perhaps, we might journey enlightened with them into a different, more human future. This would surely be a better application to download on to our mainframe selves.

Every journey they say begins with the first step, but actually it starts before then – it starts in our minds when we have the first thought, make the vague plan, fine tune it then be resolved to act on it. Then, we must prepare for the journey and every individual will need to prepare in their own way for their own particular journey. Maybe a map or plan will be required, maybe you'll have no particular destination in mind, but it's going to help if you have a goal, a place or a situation where you'd like to end up. What are the 'Summer pastures' you might travel to? You may need to consider what and whom you'll take with you. You are probably going to end up quite a different person so you'll need to consider how that will affect people who are close to you. Your journey is unlikely to be the same as theirs, that may mean you'll need to leave them behind or part company at a fork in the path at least.

I think it's fair to say that most of us who lived on the Island quickly lost touch with those who had moved away. Even with the best intentions to keep in touch somehow the connection fades and breaks. Those who leave become worlds apart. Personally, I made it a rule that I'd never go back to an old job or relationship. The only one I did keep going back to was a big, big mistake. To go back is to not move forward, it's wasting time and energy and you don't need to relearn what you've already learned – or should have learned.

If we can recognize that we have been torn away from the freedoms we once had, we have to cast off the chains we've weighed ourselves down with – otherwise we won't be going anywhere. Before we can even begin to move beyond the metaphorical prison walls, we must acknowledge that those chains are not just strong and heavy, they are chains of shining gold, they hold us down and we are forced to believe they protect us. The prison guards assure us we are safe, we are provided with all we need, here inside the walls. We are given the most glamorous toys to occupy us in our incarceration, they'll give us anything to keep us quiet, make us believe that to escape from the prison is impossible. There is only danger and death beyond the walls, they'll project any dazzling vision onto those walls to keep us from finding a window on the reality of our existence, they'll try any trick, spin any yarn, terrorise us with any threat to keep us locked away. It's your choice to stay or go.

To begin with we have to acknowledge the reality, the truth of what is happening and to do that you have to never cease to research. Don't take anyone's word as the truth, discover it for yourself, question everything, don't trust anything except your own intuition, your own gut feelings – that's why we have them. Ask yourself logically who gains, why is it happening, what is the purpose of what is happening. Where will it take us?

Ask yourself if you can live with this, will you be able to comply, or will you take another path and live with yourself?

The first thing we can do is to stop watching mainstream media TV and accepting their false narratives. It's essential to sever this chain. It's a lying grinning talk show host, it's a soap series full of disasters relieved only by the advertisements for glittering toys you'll throw away in no time at all. At its moronic best it's there to keep people passive and docile – at its worst it is an evil, deceitful propaganda machine hell bent on destroying your mind and your soul. The next thing we can do is to stop believing in politicians, religions and anyone else who tells us what to believe or what to think. Try educating yourself – it's the only way you'll get a real education.

One of the shrewdest ways for human predators to conquer their stronger victims is to steadily convince them with propaganda that they're still free...

- Dr. N.A. Scott

If you want recent history, you could try talking to those people who were around when things happened. History is always written by the winners so a first-hand account might prove worthwhile listening to. You could choose to watch You-tube – it has thousands of documentaries about every subject imaginable, you can listen to the greatest thinkers, scientists, philosophers and scholars. You can learn about anything and everything, you can watch movies from the times when they were made by creative artists - not accountants and social engineers who wouldn't know a real story, or a real drama if it hit them in the face. But, if you'd rather be distracted than enlightened you could use the miraculous technology of the Internet to play mindless games, you can fight fantasy battles, rescue fantasy princesses, fly fantasy planes, fight fantasy wars, engage in the most barbaric inhuman fantasy behaviour without ever leaving your prison cell.

You could read the books written by the prophets – books like '1984' by George Orwell, books by great thinkers and philosophers. They're not all long dead men. There are many who are alive today and you don't have to sit in dusty libraries any more. Watch the wonderful lectures of Jordan Peterson, "Read, Write and Think". Learn from the lives of people like Ram Dass, explore the wisdoms of Daoism, Buddhism, learn and keep learning. You have a wonderful mind – its capacity is limitless; you can fill it with the knowledge and wisdom of the whole of history – it's all there for free. Or you can fill it with crap – it's your choice and your mind.

The real journey, the real way to restore our true selves is to learn all we can about ourselves – how and why our minds operate. For most of us this is unexplored territory but what greater odyssey could there be than to set forth on the ultimate human journey? This is not meant to be the realm where a few privileged psychologists and philosophers go. Education is not just for the elite and the wealthy – it's everybody's right to attain as much knowledge and wisdom as they wish to. These things are now for the first time in history freely available to us. In particular, our own inner landscape is the place we all deserve to rediscover and explore, for by doing so we can learn and experience the true magnitude of the range of human experience. It is by travelling to this wonderful place that we will find true freedom and our true potential, here within ourselves we can rediscover everything that has been stolen from us.

In our distant past there were no schools to teach the young, all the knowledge and understanding they needed was passed on down from the old, the wisest to the young. Their text books were the natural world they passed through and the stories that were told around campfires. Most significantly they were provided with all they needed to know, stored within their own minds just as every other wild animal or bird comes into this world instinctively knowing how to survive. Ironically it has been the formal education of our young by institutionalised teachers over the centuries that has blanked out our natural wisdom and disconnected us from the Cosmic Interface – the connection we could plug into, the life energy source, something we all once shared. Our journey can help us return to that power source and given the right circumstances can share again – with the living Universe.

The way to acknowledge and harness this energy is to observe and contemplate it in action – then we can open our minds to accept it. You may not be able to set out on a physical journey but most of us are increasingly enjoying the benefits of time spent in the natural world, hiking, canoeing, outdoor activities, sports, adventure holidays - these are all steps in the right direction and all opportunities for discovery. Many of us now seek answers through meditation and learning about other cultural beliefs. We can now sit in a chair and read or watch a documentary to widen our horizons. These too are steps on the journey.

Above all we can spend time contemplating the natural world. Pausing on a hilltop to take in the view, watching the surf touch a beach, scanning the horizon, exploring the stars, learning the constellations, counting the bright streaks of shooting stars, recognizing the planets, watching the sunsets, the dawns letting your eyes and minds feast upon the changing colours, the ever-changing skyscapes, clouds, storms, weather. Develop an appreciation of the wonders of the natural world, soak it all into your soul. Cultivate silence in which you can hear natural sound, listen to the world around you. It speaks in many ways to your mind as well as your ears.

This life's dim windows of the soul
Distorts the heavens from pole to pole
And leads you to believe a lie
When you see with – not through the eye

\-   William Blake

Try taking a walk in the woods sometime and don't just look -   *feel*. Once you have departed from the outer world, you're taken back to a time of innocence. To walk within a wood should be a pilgrimage, not an invasion. It must be done with care and respect, moving as a fish along a stream, a deer along a narrow forest path. You must tread gently and with care so that the wood will feel your presence without alarm or fear of infection and will thereby welcome you. After all, this place is alive and everything here is connected. If you speak, or sing you should do so softly, as you would in the presence of superior creatures, for the wood is many, individual and connected to form a whole composite entity. The creatures that run and crawl across its floor, the birds that flit through its tangled tracery are as one with the whole. The earth in which the roots of the trees stand is connected to the heavens above. If you stand with them then you too are connected for each tree is like a prayer, a communication with Heaven and Earth. Go visit the woodlands - go with reverence and in the spirit of learning, for the trees have much to teach us.

There is an exciting possibility that by discovering the remote past that still exists within ourselves we may discover an alternative progression for humanity, another perspective, another possible reality, one that isn't based on fear and ignorance, one that does not require sacrifice and forever wars.

Have you ever seen the Man in the Green, heard His voice through the trees?
He sings on the wings of the wandering winds the song of a king and a queen
He lives for the good of the wild, wild wood, dies for the Spring time green
Light an oak wood fire to honour the Spirit Green

In ages past men knew my name and showed respect for me
But they closed their minds and they closed their hearts to the power that used to be
In the white moon's glow in the yew tree grove the blood of the earth flows free
Is there anyone now to know the Spirit Green?
Can you see my form in the heart of the wood and feel my breath on the breeze?
Sunlight shimmers with the gold and the green when I shake my cloak of leaves
When the sunset dies the Hunter rises, the white owl cries for me
Calling me back the song of the Spirit Green

The Spirit Green – Les Richards

I found an Island – which was indeed miraculous - but islands are very rare, so what alternatives can there be? The place you find may not be a solid, material existing place, but that's not what matters. Above all, this is a journey of the mind and the soul. You may find your Eden in a complete change of your job. You may choose to work with people who need care and help with their lives. There is real treasure buried on these human islands if you can recognize it, help them to uncover it by utilising your own experience, empathy and hard-won wisdom. It's very often the case that when you start to give yourself freely the rewards are a thousand-fold.

Everyone has a different Island to discover - if they first begin to look for it. It will be *different* from the place you know and you will know your own particular Island when you find it. Nobody can tell you where your own journey will take you or where it will end, it's for you and the Universe to decide. The good news is you won't be alone - you can do it together.

Without leaving his door he knows everything under heaven
Without looking out of his window he knows all the ways of
heaven
The further one travels the less one knows
Therefore, the Sage arrives without going
Sees all without looking, does nothing achieves everything

-    Tao Te Ching

My time in the wilderness had given me a small insight into these profound truths – truths which we almost exclusively ignore now. It seems to me we might be better off by re-learning and understanding our old ways. I wonder what future anthropologists and archaeologists will call the age we live in? The Computer Age, the Space Age? It could be the Last Age. It depends on whether we survive this next stage of human development. Extinction is always a possibility through asteroid impact or nuclear war. I suppose it depends on what they dig up – plastic probably – the Plastic Age? Hmmm, it's not an age I'd want to be included in.

The Stone Age was a sizable chunk of time – from about 2.6 million years ago until about 3,300 B.C. It's usually divided into three periods – the Palaeolithic, the Mesolithic and the Neolithic periods. The Neolithic lasted from around 4,300 B.C. to 2000 B.C. that's just 6000 years ago. Is it any wonder there is so much of the Neolithic still in us? The change from hunter gatherer to farmer was a profound turning point in our history, it happened roughly ten thousand years ago. Which is just a tiny fraction of the two million years that *homo-sapiens* have been around. However, the recent changes have come upon us with accelerating speed – the computer, the birth control pill, the view of the Earth from the Moon, the Internet and now the unknown consequences of Artificial Intelligence. It seems to me we are racing ahead before we have truly assimilated the past and learned all we can from it. Perhaps we have been deliberately denied the benefit from learning the knowledge of our past, if that is true then it's a tragedy for us – but that doesn't mean we can't rediscover and take back what is naturally ours.

Life is divided into three terms – that which was, which is - and which will be.
Let us learn from the past to profit by the present to live better in the future

- William Wordsworth

I've learned so much, far more than I could ever put into words to pass on to you. Often, I feel that this has separated me from the people in the outer world, that I am still an island surrounded by an indifferent ocean, but you cannot unlearn what you've learned, or forget what you now know. I hope these reflections will resonate with you and be useful. If you are the kind of person who asks 'why' then perhaps my words will help answer at least some of your questions. Whatever you do, keep on asking your questions, keep on exploring your inner landscape, you'll find the journey illuminating, I'm sure. Remember, this knowledge has been kept from you, this knowledge is for your development, it's your birth-right, you deserve to inherit it - but those who seek to control us, to herd us along like dumb cattle don't want us to roam freely – they want us to be controlled.

Those who control the world, the plethora of semi-secret organisations that want to imprison us in their digital gulags, their fifteen-minute cities by imposing their pseudo-religious environmental fabrications on us, their so called safe and effective medical interventions, their promises that we will 'own nothing and be happy' are the personification of evil. Our freedom, our happiness and our right to achieve our full human potential is the last thing they want for us.

What are the most valuable things I've learned? I was fortunate to have lived in a place where the remote past rubbed shoulders with the present, where the residue of the Neolithic echoed through the natural world, the seasons were real and could not be ignored, people and community - real community was made real to me, the knowledge that your behaviour, your credibility, your identity was known and respected. Your reputation precedes you and lives within you. Your credit rating has nothing to do with your bank balance; it depends on how you conduct yourself. I've also learned where we came from, why we are as we are and most unexpectedly how we might be if we can make the effort, if our destiny will be merciful to us. It takes courage to make the journey, but no price is too high to pay for the privilege of owning ourselves.

I've learned from the wonderful people I've met along the way and it's always amazed me what treasure can come from talking with the most unlikely people. It's a mistake to think that someone who might not appear to be too bright, someone who you might suppose would have nothing in common with you can't have some gift to give you. Every life has its value and you are wise to listen when you can. It's a tragedy that people feel divided by age, culture, race and circumstance. It's a tragedy that we've been silenced from sharing and communicating, but it's in our power to change that.

People don't possess ideas, ideas possess people

C.G. Jung

The rain has fallen hard at times, all night long battering on the steel roof of my boat as I lay snug and warm in my artificial burrow. The wood stove whispered comforting wisdoms in the darkness. The high water is naturally a metaphor for how life is for me at this moment, the flood of feelings, possibilities and opportunities, the strength and level of the love I share for this world, this life, the river and the woman I share it with. The world speaks, whispers its wisdoms and we who are connected can listen.

I now feel the change in me. I've spent many years of my life here on the Island. I came escaping a mad world and found sanity and peace, I found good people, all different, but all possessing a rare tolerance and a love for the Island and the river. Some stay, some move on. Is it soon going to be time for me to move on? I can't imagine finding what I've found here anywhere else, but if life has taught me anything it's that nothing is forever and I'll never say never to anything. I've served my time in the wilderness and I've learned so much, but now I have found my true home and it isn't on an island – it's with another human being. Just like the formula tells us. 3+2=5=1. A new chapter is beginning

Humankind has been sleeping, and for too long we have been dreaming a bad dream,
A dream that for untold millions, down through the centuries, has been a nightmare unending.

When we began to fall asleep, we lost our hold on the true reality, we lost our affinity with the universe, we lost our connection,
We lost the consciousness of our common collective consciousness,
We became isolated and alone and we lost sight of our place in the scheme of things,
We lost our vision and understanding, our view became narrower and obscured,
We began to see more and more of less and less.

We are now more than ever before able to communicate with our fellow beings on an unprecedented level

And yet what we are saying to each other is no more than the ramblings of those who are still not quite awake.
But those who sleep must surely awake and free themselves from the dogmatic structures and imposed beliefs that have kept them in their slumber.
People can surely become free to think for themselves and there could be at hand - a great awakening.
We could be on the brink of opening our eyes,
We might begin collecting our thoughts, remembering and re-discovering our identities
And soon, we may rise up and walk into a new day.

The Awakening – Les Richards 1995

Afterword from the Afterworld

This book is what it says on the cover – my reflections. I'm nobody's oracle but my own, so if I've said anything you disagree with then you're welcome to do your own research. If you think you recognize some of the people or places I've mentioned then please keep it to yourself – those places are gone now, so are the people and so am I.

I'm sure I must have caused some people pain in my life and for that I apologise. In recompense I hope I've given some people love, hope and what might be the best of myself.

None of us ask to come into this world and it often seems very unfair that we are forced to leave it, but I believe we must be here for a purpose. My purpose was to try and show others how wonderful and beautiful this life and this world is. It's a great pity there are so many deaf and blind idiots in it and there is so much evil - but please try to balance this out by trying your very best not to be one of them.

May the Spirit of the Universe Walk with you - L.R.

Acknowledgements

As you'll already have discovered – I'm a big fan of quotations. In fact, I've collected them in a small book for many years. Not just quotes either; I've collected anecdotes, poems, words of wisdom from all kinds of sources, from all kinds of people and I still do - although the little book is pretty much full now. I would recommend anyone to do likewise for these words have been immensely valuable to me through all the ups and downs of my wonderfully strange life. These words have been friends, counsellors and teachers. They've listened to me when nobody else would and advised me when nobody else could. So, I consider myself extremely fortunate to have carried them with me on my journey in the crumpled, dog-eared little book.

I hope none of those people I've quoted would object to being included alongside my own words. I've used some lyrics from some of the songs I've written, along with one or two of my few poems. Somebody once said that lyrics without the music read like bad poetry – that may be true, but I don't know who said that so I can't really use it as a quote.

I'd like to thank everyone who enlightened me for better or worse, everyone who shared the journey however long or briefly they walked alongside me. Most of all, I'd like to acknowledge the gift of my Universal connection which has never left my side wherever I've walked. Finally, I must give my thanks and profound gratitude for Jayne. We both had long journeys before our paths met and merged and that we now walk together has been the greatest blessing of my tangled life.

Woody